TWAIN

HUCKLEBERRY FINN

NOTES

COLES EDITORIAL BOARD

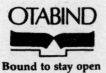

Bound to stay open

Publisher's Note

Otabind (Ota-bind). This book has been bound using the patented Otabind process. You can open this book at any page, gently run your finger down the spine, and the pages will lie flat.

ABOUT COLES NOTES

COLES NOTES have been an indispensible aid to students on five continents since 1948.

COLES NOTES are available for a wide range of individual literary works. Clear, concise explanations and insights are provided along with interesting interpretations and evaluations.

Proper use of COLES NOTES will allow the student to pay greater attention to lectures and spend less time taking notes. This will result in a broader understanding of the work being studied and will free the student for increased participation in discussions.

COLES NOTES are an invaluable aid for review and exam preparation as well as an invitation to explore different interpretive paths.

COLES NOTES are written by experts in their fields. It should be noted that any literary judgement expressed herein is just that – the judgement of one school of thought. Interpretations that diverge from, or totally disagree with any criticism may be equally valid.

COLES NOTES are designed to supplement the text and are not intended as a substitute for reading the text itself. Use of the NOTES will serve not only to clarify the work being studied, but should enhance the readers enjoyment of the topic.

ISBN 0-7740-3665-6

© COPYRIGHT 2004 AND PUBLISHED BY
COLES PUBLISHING COMPANY
TORONTO - CANADA
PRINTED IN CANADA

Manufactured by Webcom Limited
Cover finish: Webcom's Exclusive **DURACOAT**

CONTENTS

Characters

Plot 63

Structure 64

Meaning 69

Style 74

Themes in *Huckleberry Finn* 81

The Unity and Coherence of *Huckleberry Finn* 90

Mr. Eliot, Mr. Trilling, and *Huckleberry Finn* 102

Selected Criticisms 115

Bibliography 122

Samuel Langhorne Clemens (Mark Twain) Life and Works

Samuel Langhorne Clemens was born in the little town of Florida, Missouri, on November 30, 1835, shortly after his family had moved there from Tennessee. When he was about four, the family moved again, this time to Hannibal, Missouri, a small town of about five hundred people, situated on the Mississippi River roughly eighty miles north of St. Louis. In this small river-side town with large forests nearby, Clemens grew up with an attitude very much like that of Huck Finn, taking wild chances, and participating in outrageous pranks, such as rolling obstacles in front of carriages bound for church. Like Huck, he would run away from home when it suited him. And like Huck, he came to know the problems of guilt imposed by strict discipline and a rigid small-town morality.

The restrained exterior of the small community would at times open up to reveal to young Clemens a darker aspect of frontier life—sights of a murder, drunken brawls and poverty. Terror impressed itself on his dreams, and he relates that he suffered from nightmares and sleepwalking.

Clemens was charmed by the river. Rafts and steamboats travelled day and night to places a small boy could only dimly imagine. Yet in a sensitive boy this imagination could grow into a strong creative force.

When his father died in 1847, Clemens was apprenticed to a printer. He was employed for two years by the Hannibal *Courier*. Here he acquired a variety of printing and newspaper skills, for on a small-town newspaper of the pre-Civil War period, no man did simply one job. Clemens later worked for the Hannibal *Journal*, which had been founded by his older brother, Orion. His first writing was done for the *Journal*—a column, letters, replies to his own letters, and verses.

Clemens left Hannibal in 1853, at the age of seventeen, to work for a newspaper in St. Louis. This was the beginning of a lifelong pattern of travel. Clemens subsequently moved on to New York and Philadelphia. Later, he joined a brother in Muscatine, Iowa, and then managed to stay two years with his brother, Orion, in Keokuk, Iowa. It was easy for Clemens to move about as a journeyman printer, for such a worker was always needed in the printing and telegraphy trades. At twenty, Clemens had travelled more than most young men of his age. Pictures of him around this time reveal the severely intense countenance of a good-looking man with an unusually heavy growth of hair atop a clean-shaven face.

Clemens stayed one winter in Cincinnati where he firmed up his idea of going to South America for riches along the Amazon. In 1857 he started down the Mississippi for New Orleans. On the journey he met Horace Bixby, a colorful, veteran steamboat pilot. Dreams of Amazon gold were swept aside by the older and richer memories of the real river—the Mississippi. For four years Clemens worked in the pilot house of steamboats travelling up and down the Mississippi. Out of these years came source materials for his greatest books. However, he was not yet ready to write for a living even though he had contributed letters to the New Orleans *Daily Crescent*, which were signed "Quintius Curtius Snodgrass."

Growth of Writing Career

The outbreak of the Civil War ended his career on the river. Clemens had a brief tour of duty with a Confederate group at the start of the war. He soon became disillusioned with the service and withdrew from the Confederacy by going with his brother to the Nevada territory in another hope of quick wealth through silver mining. When his money ran out, he took a job for twenty-five dollars a week on the *Virginia City Territorial Enterprise*. Of particular importance at this time was his taking the pseudonym of "Mark Twain." He said that he wanted to save his critics time when they referred to him. He may have taken the name to insulate himself from unkindness. He was a terribly sensitive man, being an artist; but he loved being before the public. All that is known for certain about his pseudonym is that "Mark Twain" was a call used to pilot a riverboat. It meant no immediate danger but reason to be wary.

Mark Twain moved to San Francisco, did a short tour as correspondent in the Sandwich (Hawaiian) Islands, and became a noted lecturer around San Francisco. His friendship with men like Artemus Ward and Bret Harte, already successful literary comedians with some measure of fame, taught him that he could hold his own as a storyteller in the company of men—especially among the rough frontier society of the West. Yet he was also shrewd enough to recognize that the greater audience for these stories lay in the East. With his version of Jim Smiley and the Jumping Frog, Clemens achieved fame in the New York *Saturday Press* not long after the end of the Civil War.

Clemens broke off a successful lecture career to sail on the *Quaker City* from New York in 1866. The San Francisco *Daily Alta California* sponsored his journey to Europe and the holy land. He wrote travel letters for this paper and also for the New York *Herald* and *Tribune*. At this time he published his first book, *The Celebrated Jumping Frog of Calaveras County and other Sketches* (1867). When he returned, he revised the letters and published them as *The Innocents Abroad* (1869). In the same year he married Olivia Langdon. Olivia represented much of a dream to Clemens. Her background was of a more genteel and sensitive nature than that with which he had been associated. He regarded her tenderly and came to be governed by her often in matters of artistic taste.

It was not long before Mark Twain became firmly established as a lecturer and writer. He had found the lecture platform suited to his gifts as a skilful storyteller, and the device of letter writing permitted his thoughts to leap from one subject or one impression to another. Also, buffoonery and satire flowed easily in these forms. In *The Innocents Abroad* (1869),

Twain was outrageously funny because he could mock the previously unquestioned habits of Europeans when juxtaposed with the uninitiated consciousness of the travelling American. However, it was not his skill alone that carried Mark Twain to sudden heights of fame. He met William Dean Howells, who was then writing reviews for the *Atlantic Monthly*. The abandoned colloquialism of Twain was tempered by Howells in the choice of subject matter. Howells, of course, was soon the leader of the American literary scene and a champion of many new authors. Often Mark Twain had a tendency to become vulgar by contemporary standards; and, for better or for worse, Howells guided Twain's career with advice all through Twain's lifetime. He proofread all the important works of Mark Twain.

Clemens continued to draw upon his past travel experiences. In 1872, while living in Hartford, Connecticut, he published *Roughing It*. This narrative of his earlier days in the West featured the usual kind of hilarious exaggeration which by then had become a tradition in American literature. Mark Twain simply was better than anyone else with a tall tale, surpassing even Artemus Ward and Bret Harte. In the same year, his son Langdon died. This death began to make a pattern which deeply affected Clemens. He came to believe that all those he deeply loved would die before him. This awareness of death, always close, gave him premonitions and dark thoughts which became subjects of his last books. The nightmares of his early years now found expression.

His fame as a lecturer spread to England. He travelled there, achieving a great success. He returned to Europe several times after this to lecture and to visit. Meanwhile, he collaborated with Charles Dudley Warner in writing *The Gilded Age* (1873). Although the book is not now considered one of his best, it does have a sure vision of frontier life and feeling for deprived people, such as those who later populated the novels of Faulkner and Steinbeck.

He did not publish much for several years, sensing that "drying up" feeling not uncommon in writers. When he returned to his recollections of the Mississippi, he was able to produce seven instalments of "Old Times on the Mississippi" for the *Atlantic Monthly* in 1875. Many years later, the series provided the major portion of his successful *Life on the Mississippi* (1883). A year later he published his enormously successful book, *The Adventures of Tom Sawyer*. By now he was evidently feeling sure of his abilities and did not hesitate to return to areas where he had been successful. Out of more European travel came *A Tramp Abroad* in 1880, and *The Prince and the Pauper* in 1882. Following his *Life on the Mississippi*, he produced *The Adventures of Huckleberry Finn* in 1885.

Samuel Clemens, in addition to being a successful writer, still followed the impulses of his earlier ambition toward great wealth. He became a partner in a publishing firm called Charles L. Webster and Company. The company had some initial success but soon barely met its bills. He continued to invest in new products and inventions, some destined to be, later, cornerstones of American economy; others, merely oddities in the patent office files. However, each time Clemens was too early or too late. His deepest involvement was with the Paige typesetting machine, which cost him a fortune.

Beginning in 1891 and through 1895, Mark Twain resided in Germany, Italy, and France, with occasional business trips to the United States. The principal purpose of these business trips was to find more money for the Paige typesetter which was finally pronounced a failure in 1894. Twain ended up heavily in debt, and the Webster Publishing Company, whose profits had been poured into Paige's machine, went into bankruptcy. The year 1894 also saw the publication of *Pudd'nhead Wilson*, a more sober mining of his rural Missouri material.

In 1895-1896, Twain began an extended lecture tour through the southern hemisphere to recoup his financial losses, and at the end of this tour was able to pay his debts completely. In August of 1896, during this lecture tour, Mark Twain's favorite daughter, Suzy, died of meningitis. This year also saw the publication of what for Twain was a very serious book, *Personal Recollections of Joan of Arc*. From 1897 to 1900, the Clemenses resided chiefly in Vienna and London; *Following the Equator* was published in 1897. In 1900, *The Man That Corrupted Hadleyburg and Other Stories* was published. Twain returned to the United States, took a house in New York, and was active with Howells in an anti-imperialism campaign.

As his literary successes mounted, Mark Twain was increasingly honored by academic institutions. Yale University awarded him an honorary Master of Arts degree in 1888 and the Litt.D. degree in 1901; the University of Missouri gave him an L.L.D. in 1902; and Oxford University conferred the culminating honor with a Litt.D. in 1907.

In 1903 his wife's health began to fail, and Twain took his family to Italy. But this did not help and in 1904, in Florence, Italy, Olivia Langdon Clemens died. In 1908 Twain took up residence at Stormfield near Redding, Connecticut. Here, he spent the last few years of his life. During this period, he worked on his autobiography, with the assistance of Albert Bigelow Paine, and arranged his letters and papers. In December of 1909, his daughter Jean died, and on April 21, 1910, with the reappearance of Halley's comet, he himself died at Stormfield. Twain's life, as he himself observed, was bounded on either side by this comet. He was buried at Elmira.

Mark Twain's literary reputation has never faded. His major works have continued in print since their first publication, and numerous collections of his works, including many selective editions, have been made. Twain was always a popular writer and continues to be one. And, even during his lifetime, serious students of literature, like his friend Brander Matthews and the Scottish scholar Andrew Lang, were treating works like *Huckleberry Finn* as important literary art. Since that time, however, some academic critics have sought to regard Twain as a gifted amateur, and *Huckleberry Finn* as simply a lucky hit, while others have seen the novel as the keystone of a truly American literary tradition.

Major Publications

1867 *The Celebrated Jumping Frog of Calaveras County and Other Sketches*
1869 *The Innocents Abroad*
1872 *Roughing It*
1873 *The Guilded Age* (With C.D. Warner)
1876 *The Adventures of Tom Sawyer*
1883 *Life on the Mississippi*
1885 *The Adventures of Huckleberry Finn*
1889 *A Connecticut Yankee in King Arthur's Court*
1892 *The American Claimant*
1894 *The Tragedy of Pudd'nhead Wilson and the Comedy of Those Extraordinary Twins*
1900 *The Man that Corrupted Hadleyburg and Other Stories and Essays*
1906 *What is Man?*
1917 *Mark Twain's Letters*
1924 *Mark Twain's Autobiography*

Introduction to *Huckleberry Finn*

Inspiration and Publication

His own experiences as a youngster in Hannibal, Missouri, and his four years as a steamboat pilot on the Mississippi River, provided Samuel Clemens with the background material for the characterizations and episodes of *The Adventures of Huckleberry Finn*.

Hannibal becomes St. Petersburg in the novel. The population of Hannibal was scarcely five hundred—but Clemens preserved its character, its climate, and its people almost without transformation in *Huckleberry Finn* and other books. Tom Blankenship, the vagabond son of the town drunkard, turned into the lovable Huckleberry Finn—a boy who could not bear to be "sivilized." Clemen's mother is Aunt Polly, and his brother was the model for Sid Sawyer (Tom's brother). A long-suffering Negro, known in the slave quarters as Uncle Dan'l, became Jim—Huck's illiterate but noble companion. The Widow Douglas is a portrait of Mrs. Haliday, a widow Clemens knew. Some strolling players, in part, entered *Huckleberry Finn* as the notorious duke and king. The various farms, particularly that of the Phelps, are like that of the author's uncle, John A. Quarles, who lived near Hannibal.

During his piloting years, Clemens got to know not only every shoal and current in the mighty Mississippi, but also the people who lived and worked on it. In the time before railroads, the river provided a means of transportation for gamblers, businessmen, and sightseers up and down the twelve hundred miles between St. Louis and New Orleans.

It is believed that a series of essays Clemens wrote for the *Atlantic Monthly* in 1875, under the general title, "Old Times on the Mississippi," turned his thoughts back to his earlier life on the river and in Hannibal. In the summer of 1876 he had written several hundred pages for the book, but he found it difficult to continue. Concerning this phase in the writing of the book, Clemens wrote: "I like it only tolerably well, as far as I have gone, and may possibly pigeonhole or burn the manuscript when it is done." Clemens did in fact give the story up, and without much regret, when it was about half completed, and left it unfinished for years. A trip down the Mississippi River six years later is credited with having revived his enthusiasm in *Huckleberry Finn*, and he set to work to finish the story at a rapid pace. Clemens wrote to William Dean Howells in 1883:

> I have written eight or nine hundred manuscript pages in such a brief space of time that I mustn't name the number of days; I shouldn't believe it myself, and of course couldn't expect you to. I used to restrict myself to four and five hours a day and five days in the week, but this time I have wrought from breakfast till 5:15 p.m. six days in the week, and once or twice I smouched a Sunday when the boss wasn't looking! Nothing is half so good as literature hooked on Sunday, on the sly.

Huckleberry Finn was published almost simultaneously in London and New York in 1884—parts of it having appeared previously in the *Century Magazine*, but several last-minute corrections delayed release till early 1885. It was the first book brought out by the firm of C. L. Webster and Company, of which Clemens was a member. Even previous to its actual publication, 40,000 copies had been ordered by subscribers. E. W. Kemble illustrated the book under Clemens' direction.

Historical Context

Although the first American novel appeared as early as 1789 (*The Power of Sympathy* by William Hill Brown), the history of the novel in America is considered to begin with the nineteenth century.

In the early days, Americans simply did not have time for literature: settling and developing a virgin continent took all of their available time. Literature, after all, is a luxury, and like all aspects of culture, it demands a measure of leisure, earned by establishing mastery over one's environment. In the early days on the North American continent, mastering the environment required great physical labor, and few Americans had either the time or vitality to read literature of any complexity. Further, the Calvinist legacy of the Puritans made all non-religious literature automatically suspect: when the pioneer did read anything, he read from the Bible, *Pilgrim's Progress*, or other religious books like *Fox's Martyrs*.

On the North American continent mastery over the environment was first achieved in New England. By the end of the eighteenth century man had reached a position where he could begin to feel that he had his environment under control. His farms yielded adequate-to-good livings, and he began to have some leisure for reading. Mastery over the environment, however, did not immediately help the cause of American literature, for the English booksellers were in the wings waiting, and indeed anxious, to provide reading matter for the former colonies. The first staples of American reading were from British literature.

The first significant American men of letters in the nineteenth century were Washington Irving and James Fenimore Cooper. A group that came to be called the Brahmins was centered on Harvard College and Bowdoin College. They tended to assume that New England was the cultural center of America. Today, the prose, dramas, and verse of the Brahmins are studied primarily for historial reasons, but in their own way they controlled American literature. Men like William Dean Howells were generally regarded as outsiders and admitted into the inner circle only after a long probation.

The situation should not be over-emphasized. Emerson, for example, was one of the first to recognize and, in private, praise Whitman's *Leaves of Grass* (his sense of propriety kept his praise from being more open). The Brahmins were always searching for talent, and were ready to encourage it wherever they found it. However, they had inevitable predispositions in favor of their own group and of those who were most like them.

Into this atmosphere of snobbish gentility came a bushy-haired man of obvious talents and irrepressible vitality. In common justice, the Brahmins could not disregard Mark Twain or disdain him; but they could and always did attempt to keep him in his place. And his place, since he was unwilling to apprentice himself as Howells had done, was always below even the adopted Brahmins like Howells, until he himself had become so big that they could not disregard him. Even then, they treated his talent and accomplishments as if they were freaks of nature. His relatively unschooled vitality tended to challenge all their assumptions about literature and the writing of literature.

Literary Influences

A major influence on Clemens' work was the writings of Bret Harte. Harte's ability to supply effective settings with broad, impressionistic strokes, his ready sympathy for the downtrodden, his extravagance of dialect, and his deftness at sketching character had their counterparts in Clemens' novels. Said Clemens: "Bret Harte trimmed and trained and schooled me properly."

Another strong influence was the New Orleans writer, George W. Cable. Both he and Clemens wrote about their native regions. They were close friends and often shared the same lecture platform.

In turn, it would be difficult to estimate the number of authors who have been influenced by Samuel Clemens. He lived during a literary period that nurtured realism. Both Sinclair Lewis and Ernest Hemingway have paid tribute to Clemens for establishing the building blocks of modern American literature.

Clemens' prime importance lies in his exploration of the American literary frontier—pioneering in both style and subject matter. What he accomplished is not only expressed in the broadly democratic character of his books, but is reflected in the native works of those writers who followed him. One facet of Clemens' literary role is that his defiant attitude toward Europe helped to liberate American authors stylistically. From his time onward, America began to speak more fervently for itself through its own indigenous literature and thus to claim a place in the cultural world.

Glossary

(The following critical terms will assist the reader in understanding the discussion of *Huckleberry Finn*.)

CHARACTERIZATION: Technically speaking, characterization is anything that expounds the personality traits and characteristics of the represented character to the reader. The simplest kind of characterization would be for the narrator just to say "So-and-so was a jolly man." Obviously this provides the minimum of information that the reader needs; however, this is not the most artful or subtle way to achieve characterization. In general, most literary works develop their characterizations by a combination of several techniques. Prior to the nineteenth century it was quite common to begin with, for example, "So-and-so was a jolly man" but to then immediately follow with a demonstration; writers like Dickens used this technique. Beyond the mid-nineteenth century further subtleties began to be introduced where the narrator was required to do less and less summarizing, and characterization was developed from our watching the character in action and judging him on the basis of what he said and did. It is this kind of technique that Mark Twain uses by and large in *Huckleberry Finn*. Twain introduces his character first and then shows him to us in action, without making any real summarizations.

FIRST PERSON NARRATIVE: The novel *Huckleberry Finn* is told in the *first person*; the narrator is a character in the action and refers to himself and his own actions by use of the first person pronoun, "I." First person narrative has both virtues and problems: its great virtue is that it demands our assent to what is reported; that is to say, we cannot dispute what a first person narrator tells us because he can always appeal, as the teller of a tall story appeals, to the fact that he was there and we were not; the great drawback of first person narrative is that it is very difficult to present naturally any kind of panoramic description. In a first person narrative we are limited to what the character actually sees and what we can realistically expect him to see.

PICARESQUE: The *picaresque* narrative takes its name from the Spanish word for "rogue," *picaro*. The picaresque narrative is characterized by a loose structure which we call episodic, in many cases the thread of the narrative being held together only by the fact that each adventure happens to the same character. The thread of the narrative is often strung out on a journey and so it is somewhat common to discuss the picaresque elements in *Huckleberry Finn*. However, *Huckleberry Finn* lacks one great requirement for a picaresque novel, and that is that Huck is not a rogue. The king and the duke would make better picaresque heroes than Huck. The unity of *Huckleberry Finn* is probably better argued not from a picaresque standpoint but from a standpoint of satire and social criticism.

General and Critical Acceptance

Huckleberry Finn is now universally looked upon as one of the great American novels, but it was not always so regarded. Although popular with its readers, it was not so with the critics, partly because they denigrated subscription books, which were generally designed for the popular taste, but mainly because the critics were weaned in the school of gentility and did not know what to make of a thirteen-year-old hero who drank, smoked, told lies, and didn't like school. Consequently, most critics chose to ignore it at first.

In March, 1885, the Concord, Massachusetts, library committee ordered its exclusion on the ground that the book exerted a dangerous influence on the young. Their statement called it "rough, coarse, and inelegant, dealing with a series of experiences not elevating . . . It is the veriest trash."

9

In reporting this action, the Boston *Transcript* went on to say, "The book is so flat, as well as coarse, that nobody wants to read it . . ." and the Springfield *Republican* described its content as "harmful morality."

Even as late as 1907, Charles Whibley, writing in Blackwood's *Edinburgh Magazine*, revealed that British critics, too, could be woefully reactionary when he wrote, "The author of *Life on the Mississippi* was also the creator of Tom Sawyer and Huck Finn, two boys who will survive to cast shame upon all the humour of America."

Little by little, however, the more perceptive critics began to recognize the book's magnificent and thoroughly American tapestry. The earliest magazine review appeared in *The Century* in May, 1885. In it, T. S. Perry wrote: "Huck's virtues are an incarnation of the better side of ruffianism that is one result of the independence of Americans."

By 1891 the reception was far more positive, and one could find in an article entitled *The Art of Mark Twain*, by Andrew Lang, a number of discerning comments:

> By putting the tale in the mouth of the chief actor, Huck, Mark Twain was enabled to give it a seriousness not common in his work, and to abstain from comment. Nothing can be more true and more humourous than the narrative of this outcast boy, with a heart naturally good, with a conscience torn between the teachings of his world about slavery and the promptings of his nature . . . The world appreciates it, no doubt, but "cultured critics" are probably unaware of its singular value.

Eventually, it became apparent that *Huckleberry Finn* only *appeared* to be a juvenile book. This lucid statement by William Lyon Phelps appeared in 1907 in the *North American Review*:

> The other masterpiece, *The Adventures of Huckleberry Finn*, is really not a child's book at all. Children devour it, but they do not digest it. It is a permanent picture of a certain period of American history, and this picture is made complete, not so much by the striking portraits of individuals placed on the huge canvas, as by the vital unity of the whole composition.

Similarly, the critic John Macy wrote in 1913:

> Indeed this is more than a boy's book or a book about boys. It is a study of many kinds of society seen through eyes at once innocent and prematurely sage . . . It is a piece of modern realism, original, deep and broad, and it is in American literature deplorably solitary.

In the nineteen thirties, critics sought a social consciousness in a writer. Furthermore, they attempted to relate this awareness to his earlier life. V. L. Parrington, in *Main Currents in American Thought* (1930), notes that:

> The rebel Huck is no other than the rebel Mark Twain whose wrath was quick to flame up against the unrighteous customs and laws of caste.

The contemporary estimate of *Huckleberry Finn* may best be summed up by the following passage from *The Liberal Imagination* (1950) by Lionel Trilling:

> It is his masterpiece, and perhaps he learned to know that. But he could scarcely have estimated it for what it is, one of the world's great books and one of the central documents of American culture. *Huckleberry Finn* was once barred from certain libraries and schools for its alleged subversion of morality. The authorities had in mind the book's endemic lying, the petty thefts, the denigrations of respectability and religion, the bad language, and the bad grammar. We smile at the excessive care, yet in point of fact *Huckleberry Finn* is indeed a subversive book—no one who reads thoughtfully the dialectic of Huck's great moral crisis will ever again be wholly able to accept without some question and some irony the assumptions of the respectable morality by which he lives, nor will ever again be certain that what he considers the clear dictates of moral reason are not merely the engrained customary beliefs of his time and place.

Plot Summary

Huckleberry Finn begins as an immediate sequel to *The Adventures of Tom Sawyer*. It picks up the character of the boy Huck Finn, a riverside waif, and the son of a drunkard. Huck has shared the spotlight with Tom in the *Adventures of Tom Sawyer*, and the previous book has been split between Huck and Tom. Huck has been made a ward of the court and put out to be raised by the Widow Douglas. The new book takes over at this point, filling in a number of these details. In contrast to *Tom Sawyer*, this book is written in the first person, and we see all the characters and the action through Huck's eyes.

The first part of the book deals with a series of adventures that Huck and Tom Sawyer have around the fictional town of St. Petersburg, Missouri. This section culminates with the reappearance of Huck's father, who takes the boy off to a cabin with the idea of trying to gain control of his money. Huck, however, manages to escape, taking a canoe and heading down the river to hide from his father on an island.

On Jackson's Island, Huck joins the slave, Jim, who, for fear of being sold away, has run away from his mistress, Miss Watson. Jim is not a new character, for he has already been the butt of tricks played on him by Huck and Tom. This second section of the book relates the adventures of Huck and Jim as they float down the river on their raft, and it culminates in the incident of the Grangerford-Shepherdson feud. Chapter 19 begins a new section as Huck and Jim are joined on the raft by two confidence men who pass themselves off as a duke and a king. It is clear to Huck that these two rascals will not shrink from doing violence to him and his friend Jim. On the other hand, Jim is held in awe of their claimed nobility. Whatever their reasons, Huck and Jim accompany the duke and the king, as the two frauds bilk the country people along the Mississippi River. This section culminates when Huck, continually appalled by their schemes, finally balks at helping them cheat three orphan girls out of their inheritance. In retaliation, the duke hands Jim over to a farmer by the name of Silas Phelps, who is elated at having his hands on a runaway slave. At this point, Tom Sawyer rejoins the action and virtually forces Huck to act out a parody of the contemporary popular romances in seeking to free Jim. At the end it is revealed that Jim has been free all of this time, Miss Watson having died with a provision in her will to free Jim. All other things are righted, leaving Huck free to take off for the "territory" to escape adoption by Tom's Aunt Sally Phelps.

Characters in the Novel

HUCKLEBERRY FINN: Son of the town drunkard and narrator of the novel.

TOM SAWYER: Huck's respectable friend who delights in fantastic schemes.

WIDOW DOUGLAS: Huck's unofficial guardian who wants to civilize him.

MISS WATSON: The widow's hypocritical sister who pretends to be very pious.

JIM: Miss Watson's slave whom she plans to sell down the river.

AUNT POLLY: Tom's aunt who is also his guardian.

JO HARPER, BEN ROGERS, and TOMMY BARNES: Members of Tom Sawyer's gang.

PAP: Huck's brutal, drunken father.

JUDGE THATCHER: The kindly judge who invests money for Huck.

MRS. LOFTUS: A town lady whom Huck visits dressed as a girl.

JAKE PACKARD, BILL, and JIM TURNER: Cutthroats whom Huck discovers on a ship that is sinking.

THE GRANGERFORDS: The family who adopts Huck for a while and who are feuding with the Shepherdsons.

THE DUKE and THE KING: The two scoundrels who take over the raft for a while.

BOGGS: An offensive drunkard in a small Arkansas town who is shot down in cold blood.

COLONEL SHERBURN: The man who shoots Boggs and who later turns away the mob by ridiculing them.

BUCK HARKNESS: The man who tries to lead the mob against Colonel Sherburn.

PETER WILKS: A successful businessman with relatives in England. He has recently died and the family is waiting for the arrival of his two brothers from England.

WILLIAM and HARVEY WILKS: The two brothers who arrive after the duke and king pretend to be them.

MARY JANE, SUSAN, and JOANNA: Peter Wilks' nieces.

DR. ROBINSON and LEVI BELL: Two townspeople who see through the guise of the duke and the king.

SILAS PHELPS: The man who buys Jim for the ransom money.

AUNT SALLY PHELPS: Silas' wife, also Tom Sawyer's aunt.

Chapter by Chapter
Summaries and Commentaries

NOTE: In the original edition of the novel, Twain did not give titles to the individual chapters. In later editions, however, he did include titles, which are used here.

CHAPTER 1

I Discover Moses and the Bulrushers

Summary

Mark Twain re-establishes the character of Huck. Huck is essentially the same foundling that we have seen in *The Adventures of Tom Sawyer*, but he has now been thrown into the situation in which the Widow Douglas is attempting to "sivilize" him. We see how horribly boring it is for Huck to live with the Widow Douglas and we are taken through a whole evening with this vigorous young boy sitting in a parlor with the widow and her sister, Miss Watson. They vainly attempt to amuse him by reading him a Bible story he does not understand, and then they correct everything he does, trying to teach him how to live properly. After Huck describes all this, he tells us "I felt so lonesome I most wished I was dead." And we can believe it, for we, too, are made to feel that it would have been too much to endure. Alone in his room, Huck acts out his primitive superstitions, trying to protect himself against bad luck as a result of burning up a spider. The chapter ends as Huck hears Tom Sawyer's soft call after midnight and eagerly scrambles out his window to meet his friend.

Commentary

This short chapter immediately captures our interest by dramatizing the plight of this almost wild boy whom the Widow Douglas is attempting to tame. Both his wildness and his passionate superstition are illustrated by the incident with the spider.

The opening chapter also prepares us for Huck's coming journey, for almost every reader knows that Huck will not stay with the Widow Douglas for long. Huck's inability to fit into the Douglas household, his general restlessness and deep-seated superstition, and his eagerness to sneak out to see Tom Sawyer are vivid evidences of his intentions.

In this chapter we need to note two things about technique. First, Mark Twain makes maximum use of dialect, and yet he never confuses or frustrates the reader. This is particularly worth noting since many nineteenth-century treatments of dialect (like that of Joel Chandler Harris in his Uncle Remus stories) are almost unreadable today. Huck Finn's dialect gives the whole narrative a ring of truth. We can completely believe that these are the adventures of this kind of boy because we feel that this is the way he would have talked.

Second, we should note that Twain tells us nothing about his characters by way of formal character description. We are told that Huck was given to the Widow Douglas to be raised as her son, to be civilized, but we are told nothing about her until we see her in action; this is the keynote of Mark Twain's narrative style. He asks us to take nothing about his characters on faith; we are shown them in action, and whatever generalizations are made are withheld until we have had a chance to see them in action.

It seems hard to believe, but Huck is constantly taken in by the wild, imaginative schemes of Tom Sawyer. He almost seems a dolt in the presence of Tom's fiendish imagination. In Tom, we have the personification of much that Twain admired, the lure of status in society. Although Huck may have a primitive integrity, it is Tom who represents achievement in society. The contradictions and opposing natures of the free spirit and the one who "belongs" in his society are amply exemplified by Huck and Tom. Neither is really sufficient in this world.

CHAPTER 2

Our Gang's Dark Oath

Summary

Tom and Huck set out for the first meeting of a robber gang that Tom wants to organize. In the yard Huck stumbles and attracts the attention of Miss Watson's slave, Jim. The boys hide until Jim falls asleep. Tom decides that they need candles, and he steals back to pick them up, leaving a nickel to pay for them. He then plays a trick on Jim, lifting his hat from his head and hanging it on the limb of a tree above him. At this point Huck exercises the privilege of a first-person narrator to interrupt the story and tell us about the upshot of this trick. He tells us that, later, Jim becomes quite a celebrity among the other Negroes in the area. Jim explains that some witches had used him as a horse and ridden him all over the world. He tells them that the five-cent piece was given him by the devil as a charm to let him call up witches. Huck ends with his own comment that Jim was virtually ruined by this as a servant because he became so "stuck up." After getting the candles and playing the trick on Jim, Huck and Tom proceed to their meeting place with the other boys at the edge of a hilltop. There ensues a planning meeting in which Tom outlines to the boys what he has in mind for the robber band. After the meeting Huck returns home with his clothes "all greased up and clayey."

Commentary

This chapter contains two main points. First, we are introduced to Jim, who is to be a major character in the book. We see in Jim the same kind of passionate superstition we have seen in Huck at the end of the first chapter.

Secondly, we have Tom Sawyer and his robber band. Here Twain pokes fun at the romantic novels of Sir Walter Scott, on which Tom is obviously basing the rules for his gang. The implied thesis of this scene is that these romances act to paralyze the imagination by limiting it to certain acceptable patterns. We see this in Tom's failure to understand what ransoming is, so that we have the hilarious scene in which Tom and Ben Rogers argue about ransoming, neither of them knowing what they are talking about. Tom and the boys swear an oath in blood, and the gang is organized.

CHAPTER 3

We Ambuscade The A-rabs

Summary

Miss Watson tries to instruct Huck in prayer, but Huck see no point in praying nor does he see any evidence that it works. The character of Pap is introduced in a paragraph in which Huck remembers incidents involving his missing father. Finally, Huck tells us of several incidental "adventures," reflecting his growing dissatisfaction with being a robber who doesn't rob anything, who simply pantomimes with hog drovers, farm women, and Sunday School meetings. The chapter ends with a dialogue between Tom and Huck about the robber band in which Tom tries to defend what he is doing in terms reminiscent of Don Quixote. Huck, after deep consideration, finds this whole explanation unsatisfactory. His concluding comment on it is that "it has all the marks of a Sunday school."

Commentary

The one new element in this chapter is Pap, who figures largely in the end of this section as he tries to gain control of Huck and Huck's money. The main point of the chapter is the counterplay between the idea of prayer which Miss Watson tries to get across to Huck and the idea of enchantment that Tom tries to convey. Huck dismisses both ideas as ridiculous, and it is likely that this is a reflection of Twain's own attitude. Huck lives in a real world in which a thing either is or is not. For Huck Tom's enchanted robbers are just another of Tom's lies, to be equated with the Sunday school stories of Miss Watson. Huck is perfectly aware that both his friend and Miss Watson believe in what they are telling him, but when he puts what they tell him to the test, nothing happens. Huck looks at Tom's robber band in the same way. As far as Huck is concerned, a robber band robs and kills. When Tom's organization fails to actually rob and kill, when they have no jewelry, no gold, no prisoners to show for their efforts, Huck becomes discouraged and disillusioned. For him, this make-believe, which is very entertaining to Tom, is simply a fiction—an outright lie.

16

CHAPTER 4

The Hair-Ball Oracle

Summary

The chapter opens with Huck's account of his slow adjustment to the ways of the Widow Douglas and Miss Watson, and of his grudging acceptance of school. Then, one day, he sees some curious boot tracks in the snow and recognizes them as Pap's. Fearful of Pap's intentions, Huck runs to Judge Thatcher and signs away his money, for a "consideration" of one dollar. Huck then goes to consult Jim, the superstitious Negro, who has a hair-ball that he uses for conjuring. The nonsense that Jim gives to Huck in answer to his questions about the future are a model of the superstitious double-talk that lies behind fortunetelling and conjuring. The chapter ends as Huck returns to his room, more or less reassured by the ambiguities of Jim's fortunetelling, only to find Pap waiting for him.

Commentary

The first motif in this chapter is Huck's partial adjustment to his life with the Widow Douglas. We are treated to details such as Miss Watson's not letting Huck throw salt over his left shoulder, and we must note here the way the Widow Douglas and Miss Watson work at odds: Miss Watson attacking and challenging Huck, the Widow Douglas defending him. The widow is most understanding. It is Miss Watson who bothers Huck. Where the widow patiently waits for change in Huck, Miss Watson looks for more immediate results. The widow operates with heart, and Miss Watson works with the intellect.

The second incident, Huck's finding the boot print and "instinctively" reacting to prevent Pap from getting control of his money, is an example of instinctive wisdom on Huck's part that will loom ever larger as the narrative proceeds. We also see the first of many parallels that Twain draws between Huck, the waif for whom civilization is only a veneer, and Jim, the illiterate slave. Both exhibit the shrewd common sense of those who observe the world exclusively in terms of their own experience, combined with a fervent belief in superstitious mumbo jumbo.

CHAPTER 5

Pap Starts in on a New Life

Summary

In the book's first physical description of a character, Huck tells us what his father looks like. Pap expresses his strong disapproval of Huck's appearance and clothing and forbids him to go back to school. After Huck denies that he has any substantial amount of money, Pap takes the dollar that Judge Thatcher had given Huck and goes off to get drunk.

Pap next tries to force Judge Thatcher to give him Huck's money, and the judge retaliates by going to court in an attempt to have himself and the Widow Douglas declared Huck's legal guardians. The court judge is new, however, and refuses to take Huck away from Pap. In a high comic scene, the new judge takes Pap into his house where he and his wife are elated by Pap's tearful promises to reform. The "reformation" lasts only a few hours, for during the night Pap sneaks out for a bottle and gets himself roaring drunk in the judge's guest room.

Commentary

The principle of this chapter is Huck's implicit assumption that Pap and others like him cannot be reformed. Notice the new judge's conclusion—which Huck apparently accepts, for he repeats it—that Pap might be reformed with a shotgun, but in no other way. In Huck's world, as Huck describes it for us, the governing notion is deterministic: what man is today, he will continue to be tomorrow. Thus we should not regard Huck himself as reformed simply because *he* is becoming acclimated to schooling and being civilized by the Widow Douglas. Given enough time, a new behavior pattern might be established, or at least that possibility is suggested by Huck's partial adjustment, but we are never allowed to believe that Huck has undergone as profound an experience as reformation. By making it apparent that Huck has not really been converted to civilization, Twain prepares us for his coming escape and journey down the river.

CHAPTER 6

Pap Struggles with the Death Angel

Summary

Pap sues Judge Thatcher to get control of Huck's money. Impatient at the slow process of law, he catches Huck and takes him from St. Petersburg across to the Illinois side of the river, where he locks him in an old cabin. Here Huck is a virtual prisoner for two months or more, during which time his fancy manners and clothes are quickly forgotten. Huck welcomes his return to his old ragtag, bobtail life; but he does object to Pap's tendency to whip him whenever he is feeling the least bit ornery. As Pap's adventures with the law drag on inconclusively, he beats Huck with increasing frequency and Huck begins to think about escaping. In this chapter we are treated to Pap's drunken tirade against the government, which he blames for all his troubles. He is particularly incensed by his encounter with a free and obviously well-educated Negro. The tirade ends with Pap tumbling head over heels into a tub of salt pork. Continuing his drinking after supper, Pap lapses into a stupor. Later, Huck is awakened when Pap has a fit of delirium tremens. Pap imagines Huck to be the Angel of Death come for him and attacks him with a clasp knife. Huck escapes, and after the old man passes out, Huck finally dozes off with a loaded rifle set to protect himself.

Commentary

There are two essential motifs in this chapter. First, we see the sense of relief Huck experiences at his return to his former way of life: loafing, hunting, fishing, and generally doing nothing. He is even willing to accept an occasional beating as the price of what he regards as freedom, despite his imprisonment. It is only when the beatings become frequent that he objects.

The second motif is the bitter ridicule to which Twain subjects the class of "poor white trash" represented by Pap. In his drunken, unreasoning tirade, Pap blames everyone but himself for his troubles. His reaction to the free "nigger" is particularly significant: no matter how low his status, he has always been able to look down on the race of slaves, but here is a member of the race who has obviously achieved more than he has. Although Huck, of course, completely accepts the institution of slavery and regards all Negroes as just "niggers," this incident is often thought to be an indication of Twain's own attitude.

CHAPTER 7

I Fool Pap and Get Away

Summary

When Pap wakes up he does not remember his attack on Huck. Huck explains the loaded rifle by telling Pap that someone tried to break in during the night, then Huck goes to see if there are any fish on the lines. Down at the river he discovers a canoe which he secures and hides from Pap. He then goes over to the "trot lines" and pulls them up to find that they have caught catfish which he takes back to the cabin for breakfast. About noon Pap notices a log raft floating down the river. He catches it and takes it to town to sell the logs. Huck decides to escape and sets the stage by making it appear that someone has broken in and killed him, taking elaborate pains to indicate that a fight and robbery have taken place. He takes a load of supplies, hops in the canoe, and floats down to Jackson's Island, a few miles downstream from Pap's cabin. Hiding his canoe under some willow branches, he goes to sleep on the bank.

Commentary

One of the things to note in this chapter is Twain's descriptive technique. We are not directly told that the cabin has a dirt floor until Huck sets the scene for his "murder" with the blood from a wild pig. At that point we learn that the pig is bleeding on the ground, that the floor of the cabin is not board, but simply hard-packed earth. Earlier we had learned other details about the cabin, not as an author would stand apart and describe it to us, but as these details occur naturally in the course of the narrative. It is this fluidity of description which makes *Huckleberry Finn* a unique work of art and helps to set Mark Twain apart from other great American writers of his time. To the author goes credit for restraining his journalistic eye for detail and for injecting these details only when his narrator, Huck, would naturally use them.

We should also note Huck's comment that he wishes Tom Sawyer were around to advise him on throwing in the "fancy touches." In this, of course, he is mistaken. Tom Sawyer's "fancy touches" would have given everything away as phony: the very success of Huck's "death" depends upon Huck's pure common sense in setting the scene. In the earlier chapters, and later on in the Phelps farm episodes, Huck considers Tom Sawyer's judgment superior to his; yet Huck is right much more often than Tom. Here again we see how Twain regards native common sense as superior to the romantic illusions of nineteenth-century English literature.

CHAPTER 8

I Spare Miss Watson's Jim

Summary

The next day on the island Huck watches as a steamboat travels up and down trying to find his drowned body. From his hiding place Huck sees most of the people he knows standing by the rail, watching for Huck's body to appear when a cannon is fired. Finally the boat goes back to St. Petersburg and Huck settles down to life on the island. While exploring one day, he discovers Jim, Miss Watson's slave. Jim has come to the island because he feared he was in danger of being sold "down to Orleans." He has slipped away on a day that the two women were going off to a camp meeting, the other slaves being in effect on holiday, and has floated down the river on a raft to Jackson's Island. Jim is at first afraid of Huck because he thinks Huck is a ghost. Jim, like everyone else, has believed Huck to be dead. Then Huck and Jim compact to live for a while on the island, and they settle down and begin one of a number of long talks. Huck is impressed by the extent to which Jim knows the "signs" in folklore, and he informally sets about learning more superstition from Jim.

Commentary

In this chapter the themes of natural wisdom and popular superstition are tightly interwoven. We see the effect of superstition on such otherwise civilized types as Judge Thatcher, Widow Douglas, and Tom Sawyer, who believe that devices such as floating bread and shooting off cannons will help to recover Huck's body. We are then treated to a further exposition of Huck's superstitions, followed by an even longer catalogue of Jim's folk beliefs.

Running as a counterpoint to this chronicle of human foolishness is the natural wisdom that both Huck and Jim show in getting to the island and escaping detection. The two themes come to a head at the end of the chapter, in the dialogue about Jim's "wealth" and his reading of the signs; but even here it is worth noting that Jim's ignorant speculations are larded with common sense and shrewd observations.

CHAPTER 9

The House of Death Floats By

Summary

Jim and Huck settle down to housekeeping in a cave on Jackson's Island. In the course of their adventures they catch a raft which enables them to loot an old frame house that is floating down the river. In this house they find the body of a man who has been shot in the back. Jim tells Huck not to look at the face because "it's too gashly." Huck does not protest. Then they pick up whatever they can find, operating with all the selectivity of pack rats. In addition to some useful things, they haul off a wooden leg, an old fiddle bow, a dog collar, a horseshoe, and other such trash. Loaded down with their "treasures," they return safely to the island and haul their catch into the cave.

Commentary

The relationship between Huck and Jim, starting on the island and continuing during their journey down the river, has been commented on by a number of critics. Leslie Fieldler, in his controversial and often eccentric book *Love and Death in the American Novel* (1960), argues that the relationship between Huck and Jim amounts to a rejection of normal sexuality in favor of one of the many possible and not necessarily unnatural relationships between two males. Fiedler seems to suggest that any novel which does not have a full-bodied woman in it is automatically exposed to a charge of avoiding the representation of normal heterosexual human relationships. When applied to *The Adventures of Huckleberry Finn*, the point is not well taken. Huck is, after all, a boy on the early edge of adolescence, who has in addition cut himself loose from normal human society. As such, it would be inappropriate for him to have a female companion on his journey down the river, and his chronological age would tend to prohibit the possibility of contacts with girls or women on shore as he passes by. One could more convincingly argue that in minimizing Huck's interest in girls at this stage of his life Mark Twain preserved the situational integrity of his narrator.

We should also note how, by introducing the dead man at this point, Twain plants a detail to which he will make crucial reference at the end of the narrative.

CHAPTER 10

What Comes of Handlin' Snakeskin

Summary

After they return to the cave, Jim won't allow Huck to talk about the dead man, saying that bad luck will come if they do. Huck refers to their finding a snakeskin which is also supposed to be an omen of bad luck, and challenges this belief in terms of their "truck" and the eight dollars in silver they had found in some of the clothes. Jim's answer is that they should wait and see. Later in the week Huck finds and kills a rattlesnake and plants it in Jim's bed as a joke. When Jim climbs into bed at night the rattlesnake's mate is there, and bites him. Huck, under Jim's instruction, doctors Jim according to folk wisdom, and after about four days Jim begins to recover. Huck agrees that handling the snakeskin had, indeed, brought bad luck. A few days later they catch a huge catfish which, Jim says, would be worth a good deal if they could sell the meat.

The next day Huck is restless and wants to sneak into town to find out what is going on. Jim suggests that Huck dress up as a girl, so they fix up one of the gowns they had taken from the floating house and Jim coaches Huck in how to pass himself off as a girl. Huck canoes into St. Petersburg, where he peeps into the window of a shanty at the edge of town. He realizes that the woman sitting inside is a newcomer, so he decides to knock at the door to try to get some information.

Commentary

The bulk of this chapter is a continuation of the superstition *vs.* natural wisdom theme. Huck's commen sense forces him to question the snakeskin superstition, but he changes his mind after the rattlesnake bites Jim. Huck, of course, chooses to ignore his own lapse of good sense in putting the dead rattlesnake at the foot of Jim's bed. Jim would probably not have made such a mistake. In this connection, note the continuing evidence of Jim's knowledge of natural phenomena—he points out that the ball in the belly of the catfish must have been there a long time because it is so heavily coated. On the other hand, his superstitious remedies for snakebite certainly do not contribute to his recovery.

This chapter also signals the end of the island interlude. Chapters 8, 9, and 10 have been a kind of interruption of the narrative, but they have served the purpose of establishing the relationship between Huck and Jim, telling us a great deal about their characters. This technique of departing from the main line of the story to record an interesting vignette or make a characterization more vivid is one of the hallmarks of Twain's style. At the end of the chapter he skilfully draws us back into the narrative as Huck stands hesitantly outside the house in St. Petersburg.

CHAPTER 11

They're After Us!

Summary

When the woman opens the door, Huck presents himself as a girl named Sarah Williams from a town seven miles away. The woman invites Huck in and tells him about the death of Huckleberry Finn! She says that most of the townspeople at first had believed that Pap, who has since disappeared, had killed Huck, but that many now think that Jim is the murderer—that in fact there is a $300 reward for Jim's capture. The woman tells Huck that she has seen smoke on Jackson's Island and that her husband is about to go there to search for Jim. To hide his nervousness, Huck attempts to thread a needle. The woman's suspicions are aroused by the way Huck handles the needle and thread, and she asks him his name once more. This time Huck says it is Mary Williams. The woman then puts Huck to a series of tests, such as throwing a bar of lead at a rat and catching something in his lap, which convince her that he is really a boy. When she confronts Huck and tells him she thinks he is a runaway apprentice, he admits it at once and makes up another, much more convincing story. The woman, who tells Huck her name is Judith Loftus, believes he is telling the truth in most respects and promises to befriend him. Huck rushes back to the island where he builds a decoy fire and then routs Jim out of bed so that they can load their raft and take off down the river.

Commentary

This chapter is particularly noteworthy for the swift, sure portrait that Twain draws of a frontier woman. Judith Loftus, who undoubtedly has had little formal education, possesses common sense and genuine intuition. She is hospitable, warmhearted, and not easily fooled. This characterization is another indication of the value Twain placed on the qualities of ordinary folk.

This episode also highlights another facet of Huck's character—his capacity for lying. When he is exposed in the difficult role as a girl, he slips easily into another lie that is good enough to fool the shrewd Mrs. Loftus. Huck uses his skill at lying as a shield to hide his real identity. This device, together with his tendency simply to report events rather than pass judgment on them, permits him to function as an essentially neutral character: an ideal commentator on the society he encounters in his journey along the river. The disguise is a favorite device of Mark Twain and has been used before in *Tom Sawyer*.

CHAPTER 12

Better Let Blame Well Alone

Summary

Huck and Jim float down the river until just before dawn, when they hide the raft and lie low during the day. That night Jim rigs the raft with a wigwam for shelter and builds a dirt pit in the middle of the wigwam to serve as a firebox. They continue their journey during the next several nights, observing the peaceful panorama of the sky and river and the lights of the towns on shore. When they pass St. Louis, Huck tells us "it was like the whole world lit up." Occasionally Huck slips into a town to make small purchases from a store or to "borrow" a chicken or some vegetables from a farm. He and Jim ease their consciences about this "borrowing" by agreeing to refrain from taking certain items from time to time, although the items they choose to eliminate are not likely to be found at that time of year.

On the fifth night, after a storm, they sight a wrecked steamboat which Huck wants to board, against Jim's advice. Huck wins Jim over, but when they climb on board they hear angry voices. Jim heads back for the raft as Huck, in a classic eavesdropping scene, sneaks forward and overhears two cutthroats agree to murder a third whom they are holding prisoner. In a panic, Huck rushes to find Jim, only to discover that the raft has broken loose and they are marooned on the boat with the gang of murderers.

Once they board the wreck, the mood changes abruptly to one of suspense and terror. Huck's boyish curiosity and adventurousness overcome Jim's reasonable fears, and as a result the two find themselves in mortal danger. Twain leaves us anxiously waiting to discover what will happen next.

Commentary

Few chapters in American literature show as much contrast in mood as this one does. The opening pages have a high lyric quality as Huck describes the scene as they float down the river during the night: "It was kind of solemn, drifting down the big still river, laying on our backs looking up at the stars, and we didn't ever feel like talking loud, and it weren't often that we laughed only a little kind of a low chuckle." Huck and Jim, represented here as "children of nature," are touched by the mystic solemnity of the night sky. This is reminiscent of Whitman's "When I Heard the Learned Astronomer," where a similar attitude is reflected. Again, as they pass the little towns, Huck describes them: "Every night we pass towns, some of them way up on black hillsides, nothin' but just a shiny bed of lights, not a house could you see."

The name of the wrecked steamboat, we learn, is the *Walter Scott*. The name of the boat is exceedingly important for what it represents. Mark Twain had a strong aversion to the world of the author Walter Scott and constantly derided his work. To Mark Twain, the stories of kings and their followers who trespassed on the rights of others were miserable misrepresentations of true romance. He saw kings and their kind as murderers and thieves. Hence, the present crew of the *Walter Scott* truly belong there.

CHAPTER 13

Honest Loot from the *Walter Scott*

Summary

Huck and Jim watch as the two cutthroats load their skiff with loot from the wreck, planning to leave the third behind to drown. When the two scoundrels go off to strip their former comrade, Huck and Jim jump into the skiff and cut it loose. Slipping down the river, Jim and Huck manage to find the raft. Then Huck gets off at the first landing they pass. There he wakes the ferry operator and tells him a cock-and-bull story about his (Huck's) father, mother, and sister, claiming they are stranded on the steamboat wreck with the niece of the wealthiest man in the area. The ferry captain rousts out his engineer and takes off to rescue any survivors. Soon the steamboat wreck comes floating down the river, but it is evident that there is no life on board. Huck rejoins Jim near dawn and they turn in for a badly needed sleep.

Commentary

Huck's ability to concoct a plausible story out of whole cloth reaches its height in this chapter. His invention of "Miss Hooker," the "niece" of the wealthy Mr. Hornback, is a stroke of sheer genius, for it is evident that the ferry operator would not have ventured out into the river without this extra touch.

Notice also how the Widow Douglas has had a strong influence on Huck. His motive for sending the ferry to the rescue is that the widow would have been proud of him, "because rapscallions and deadbeats is the kind the widow and good people takes the most interest in." Miss Watson's righteous lectures have had little effect on Huck, but Widow Douglas, by her kindness and good example, has done much to mold his character.

CHAPTER 14

Was Solomon Wise?

Summary

After they awake from their heavy sleep, Huck and Jim tally up the profits from their adventure on the wrecked steamboat. They conclude that each of them is richer than he has ever been in his life, and they spend that day lazing around in the woods and smoking some of the captain's cigars. Huck reads to Jim from some books they have found on the boat—books having to do with kings and earls and dukes and such—and Jim is fascinated by this picture of another way of life. The discussion turns to the story of King Solomon and the two women who claim to be the mother of the same child. Jim insists that anyone who wants to cut a child in two cannot be called wise. The truth, Jim maintains stubbornly, is that Solomon had so many children he didn't care about one more or less. Then they shift subjects and talk about languages. Huck cannot communicate to Jim the problems of foreign languages, Jim assuming that all people talk the same way he does. Huck ends the discussion in a fit of mild disgust.

Commentary

The dialogue between Huck and Jim in this chapter is not only a comic feat of skills but is also an illustration of Twain's belief in both the power and limits of natural wisdom. In his disapproval of Solomon's decision, and especially in his failure to understand how anyone could speak a different language, Jim demonstrates a childlike inability to deal with abstract concepts. On the other hand, Huck, despite having had some education, cannot cope with the force of Jim's arguments; he has to fall back on his supposed superiority as a white man to make up for his defeat.

CHAPTER 15

Fooling Poor Old Jim

Summary

Proceeding down the river toward Cairo pronounced (Kay-ro), Huck and Jim run into a heavy fog. Huck, in the canoe, tries to tie the raft to a towhead (a sand bar covered with cottonwood), but he misses the tie, and the raft, caught in a stiff current, shoots on without him. Huck whooping and occasionally hearing a distant answer, wanders along the river until the fog lifts. Finally he comes upon the raft, which is battered and covered with leaves and rubbish, and finds that Jim is asleep. Huck quietly lies down and pretends to wake as if he had never been gone. He insists that Jim must have dreamed the whole episode about their separation in the fog. Jim at first seems to believe Huck and begins a lengthy interpretation of the "dream," predicting that they are finally going to get to the free state. When Huck points to the leaves and rubbish that the raft has picked up and asks Jim how he interprets those things, Jim makes a painfully sharp speech about how worried he was when Huck was lost, and says that the leaves and rubbish are trash, like people who try to make fools of their friends. Huck, humiliated by Jim's reproach, apologizes to his companion.

Commentary

Huck's attempt to play a trick on Jim can be explained by his boyish thoughtlessness and his annoyance at being out-argued by Jim in the previous chapter, but it is also a reflection of his conditioning by the slave-holding society of the Mississippi Valley. Although many slaves, particularly household servants like Jim, were treated with kindness by their masters, they were regarded principally as property. They were seldom given credit for emotions like those of other human beings. Thus Huck, who has come to value Jim as both a friend and an advisor, is capable of ignoring Jim's obvious joy at finding that Huck is alive in order to carry out a petty deceit. When Jim reveals the depth of his emotion, Huck realizes for the first time that Jim is a complete person and vows never to hurt him again. This does not mean that Huck is won over to Abolitionism—he still thinks that helping a runaway slave is wrong—but he has been forced into an awareness of genuine human relationship, and the stage is set for his loyalty to Jim in later chapters, even though it is put to several severe tests.

CHAPTER 16

The Rattlesnake-Skin Does its Work

Summary

As Huck and Jim proceed down the river, Jim anticipates reaching Cairo and making the turn up the Ohio toward the free states. Every time they see a light he jumps up yelling "Dah she is!" The closer they come to Cairo, the more Huck begins to worry. After all, Jim is a runaway slave, and he, Huck, is helping him. The more Huck thinks about it the worse he feels. Then Jim says that once he gets to the free states, he will save his money to free his wife, and then, if necessary, steal his children into freedom. This upsets Huck and he finally determines to hop in the canoe and find somebody who will capture Jim. Soon he is hailed by two men in a skiff who are looking for other runaway slaves, but Huck cannot carry out his resolution. When they begin to get suspicious of his raft, Huck tells the men a story which leads them to suspect that his father is on the raft sick with the smallpox. They float a piece of wood down to him with two twenty-dollar gold pieces on it and let him go on his way. Huck, still morally confused, returns to the raft, where Jim exults over how good Huck is and how much help he has been. They continue, still not finding Cairo, until finally, in the daylight, they see the clear Ohio water running into the muddy water of the Mississippi. This sign tells them that they have already floated beyond Cairo. They sail on looking for a chance to buy a canoe to go back up river.

During the night the raft is sunk by an upstream boat that apparently does not see their light. Huck and Jim dive for the bottom, and when Huck comes up he cannot find Jim. He paddles for shore, the Kentucky bank, where he finds an old-fashioned double log house. Here he is cornered by a pack of dogs and has to wait for someone to come and call them off.

Commentary

In this chapter we see the extent to which Huck's mind is dominated by the mores of a slave-holding society. There is a head-on clash between his belief in what he has been taught and his natural humanitarian inclination.

When the chips are down, Huck chooses humanity, but he still thinks he has done wrong. Huck puts it this way:

> They went off, and I got aboard the raft, feeling bad and low, because I knowed very well I had done wrong, and I see it warn't no use for me to try to learn to do right; a body that don't get started right when he's little ain't got no show—when the pinch comes there ain't nothing to back him up and keep him to his work, and so he gets beat.

Here we see Twain's ironic view of a society whose values are so twisted that right and wrong are indistinguishable. Twain himself was very much a rebel, and so he has his alter-ego, Huck, cope with society's distorted value structure by rejecting it completely.

Twain had difficulties with his plot in this chapter and abondoned work on the book in 1876. He resumed work on it some six years later.

In the original manuscript Mark Twain had a long "Raftsman Passage" included in Chapter 16. It was deleted in the final, published version. It can, however, be found in Chapter 3 of *Life on the Mississippi*.

CHAPTER 17

The Grangerfords Take Me In

Summary

When the Grangerford family, whose house Huck has stumbled upon in the Kentucky swampland, is awakened by the barking dogs and discovers Huck, the boy invents a story about being lost. The family at first treats him as if he were an intruder into a military camp, but satisfied that he is not a "Shepherdson," they let him in and feed him. He settles down to live with them for a while. The house is furnished in a kind of tacky elegance that impresses Huck. He is particularly attracted to some pictures and verses created by a deceased daughter of the family. Huck enjoys living with the Grangerfords, especially because they have good food and "just bushels of it too!"

Commentary

The Grangerfords' quick acceptance of Huck, once they have determined he is not a Shepherdson, is characteristic of frontier hospitality which acted to equalize all men.

Huck's fascination with the Grangerford house permits Twain to compose an elaborate description, a relatively rare thing in his work. Twain has a specific purpose, however, for the style in which the Grangerford home is furnished could best be characterized as "back country miscellaneous." The painting and poetry of the dead Grangerford daughter, Emmeline, provides Twain with a chance to parody the art and verse of Julia A. Moor, called "The Sweet Singer of Michigan," which Twain detested. Note that Huck himself expresses no such opinion; indeed, he likes Emmeline's work. Once again, he functions as the essentially neutral commentator on the world around him. The absurdities are apparent only to the reader.

CHAPTER 18

Why Harney Rode Away for his Hat

Summary

Huck continues his description of the Grangerford family and their genteel ways. The family is quite wealthy, and everyone, including Huck, has a personal servant. Huck becomes particularly friendly with the youngest son, Buck, as both are about the same age. The Grangerford boy tells Huck about the feud with the Shepherdsons which has been going on for thirty years. Buck has no idea how the feud started, but accepts without question the proposition that all male Grangerfords and Shepherdsons are inalterably committed to killing one another. The following Sunday after church, where the Grangerfords and the Shepherdsons have listened to a sermon on brotherly love, Sophia, the younger Grangerford daughter, sends Huck back to the church to get her Bible. Huck finds in the Bible a strange note that apparently has great meaning to Sophia. That afternoon Huck's servant, Jack, offers to show him a stack of water moccasins in the swamp. When Huck reluctantly follows Jack to the swamp he finds Jim hiding there. The Grangerford slaves have been feeding and protecting Jim and have also found the raft, which Jim has outfitted. Huck and Jim make plans to move along shortly.

When Huck awakens the next day everything is in confusion. Jack tells him that Miss Sophia has run off with Harney Shepherdson and that all the Grangerfords have gone to bring her back. In the pitched battle that follows, part of which Huck witnesses, all the Grangerford men, including Buck, and some of the Shepherdsons are killed. Huck sorrowfully covers Buck's face and then, with relief, joins Jim on the raft. His closing observation is: "You feel mighty free and easy and comfortable on a raft."

Commentary

The Grangerford-Shepherdson feud is Twain's satiric commentary on the Montague-Capulet feud in *Romeo and Juliet* and on the romantic traditions of the old South. These two families, who conduct themselves in accordance with the genteel standards of the Southern aristocracy, nevertheless proceed mindlessly to kill one another for a vague reason that is itself rooted in the traditions of the Southern frontier. Twain, of course, respects the frontiersman's warmth, hospitality, and independence, but has little regard for the code of chivalry romanticized in so much fiction of the period.

Huck, himself, sees none of this. To him the Grangerfords are a wholly admirable family. Although he does not necessarily accept the validity of the feud, he records Buck's explanation without comment. It is only when he is confronted by the horror of the death of his friends that he expresses regret at the loss of human life. Indeed, he is deeply moved by the death of Buck. Child of nature that he is, however, Huck easily shakes off his sorrow and returns with Jim to the free and easy life on the river.

CHAPTER 19

The Duke and the Dauphin Come Aboard

Summary

The two runaways resume their idyllic life on the river. For a few days, they float along on the raft with few incidents, simply enjoying their freedom and laziness. One morning Huck finds a canoe and paddles over to shore where he encounters two men who are being chased by dogs and horsemen. Huck helps them escape by bringing them to the raft. In the conversation that follows, it becomes apparent that the newcomers, who do not know each other, are roving confidence men. After a time, the younger one says that he has a sad story to tell and proceeds to represent himself as the Duke of Bridgewater, fallen upon hard times. Not to be outdone, the elder then claims to be the Dauphin, true King of France. The younger one is clearly displeased at being outclassed by his fellow bunko artist in their game of "one-upmanship," but the elder quickly smoothes his ruffled feelings. The chapter ends with Huck's observation that he knew from the first that they were not nobility.

Commentary

The king and the duke are vivid examples of a familiar back-country type, the roving confidence man and medicine-show operator. Notice the range of things that the duke and the king say they do: from selling fake patent medicine "guaranteed" to take tartar off teeth, to running revivals, to journeyman printing, to dramatic acting. The two are sharply contrasted not only in age and physical appearance, but also in their way of speaking and general attitudes. The duke seems to have been less successful in his schemes, perhaps because, having learned a craft, he has acquired a bit of honesty. The king, on the other hand, is quicker-witted and, as we shall see, is able to improvise more easily to take advantage of a sudden opportunity.

Note also Huck's statement in the last paragraph that he recognized immediately that the two men are of the same type as Pap, and that the best way to get along with them is to let them have their own way. Huck is the realist who, as much as possible, avoids judging the moral standards of others.

CHAPTER 20

What Royalty Did to Parkville

Summary

The duke and the king suspect that Jim is a runaway slave, so Huck makes up another of his tall stories to account for Jim and the fact that they have to hide during the day. The duke then says that he will figure out a way for them to travel during the day. That night the two confidence men take the beds in the wigwam, leaving Huck and Jim to stand watch as the raft resumes its journey.

The next day, as they again wait in hiding, the duke and the king lay plans to raise some money. The duke suggests that he and the king put on a performance of scenes from *Romeo and Juliet* and *Richard the Third*. After dinner they come to a little town which the king and the duke decide to scout. Huck goes along to get some supplies. The town is practically deserted; everyone has gone off to a camp meeting. Huck and the king leave the duke in the local printing office and go off to the meeting, which turns out to be a well attended revival. The king proceeds to shout and sing so loudly that he can be heard above everybody else. He works his way up to the platform and launches into a sermon in which he represents himself as a reformed pirate whose only desire is to preach the gospel to other pirates. Everyone, including the king, bursts into tears and someone yells for him to make a collection. The king needs no urging. He passes among the crowd blessing everyone and kissing the women as they put money in his hat. Then he and Huck return to the raft. The king's take totals $87.75, plus a three-gallon jug of whiskey that he'd found under a wagon. However, the duke, who had set up business in the printshop and sold some newspaper subscriptions to a few local farmers, has collected only $9.50! The duke has also taken the time to run off a poster offering a reward for a runaway slave, whose decription fits Jim. He says they can use this to claim that they have captured Jim and are taking him down to New Orleans to return him to his owners. In this way they can travel in daylight and tie Jim up if they meet anyone. That night, after the duke and the king have drunk themselves to sleep, Jim observes to Huck that he can stand one or two kings but hopes they don't meet any more.

Commentary

Huck's account of the revival meeting is one of Twain's finest descriptive passages. Using a technique that in a contemporary novelist would be consciously cinematic, Twain has Huck's "narrative eye" rove unerringly over the proceedings. He describes the way people are dressed, what they are doing, and how they respond. Finally, he focuses tightly on the preacher and his sermon, and the description gives way to the preacher's speech.

We should also note at this point that up to the arrival of the king and the duke on the raft, there has been a marked contrast between the idyllic life on the river and the hypocrisy and evil Huck has encountered on shore. Now the evil in the towns has infested the raft, but it is Jim who expresses his dissatisfaction.

In addition to making the king and the duke into swindlers, Mark Twain further delights in giving them no names but those of royalty. To Mark Twain's mind, the duplicity of the pair is no worse than that of kings and dukes anywhere. The outrage that Huck feels against the real royalty of this world is transfigured in the outrages performed by the duke and the king. Even though Huck's knowledge of kings is historically inaccurate, he knows what he feels about royalty. It does not take Jim long to regret his own closeness to royalty.

CHAPTER 21

An Arkansaw Difficulty

Summary

As they float down the river the duke coaches the king in the Shakespearean scenes they plan to do. The duke manages to have some playbills printed, and they prepare to put on a show at the next opportunity. At an Arkansas town, a circus is to be presented that afternoon, so the duke rents the courthouse for an evening performance. After putting up the playbills, they decide to poke around the town. Huck gives us a detailed description of the houses and people. Just before noon, a back-country character named Boggs gallops into town for his monthly "drunk." One of the local loafers assures Huck that, although Boggs is given to cursing and threatening anyone in sight when he is drunk, in reality he is completely harmless. Boggs' particular target this month is the wealthy Colonel Sherburn, who warns Boggs that he will tolerate being abused until just one o'clock; but that if Boggs mouths one more insult after that, he, Sherburn, will hunt him down. The townspeople vainly try to quiet Boggs, but a few minutes past the deadline, Sherburn cold-bloodedly shoots him down. For a while the town loafers are diverted by a re-enactment of the killing. Then somebody says that Sherburn should be lynched. The chapter ends with the townspeople collecting clothes lines to use as hanging rope.

Commentary

This chapter and the one that follows are among the most bitterly satirical passages in Twain's work. With a meticulous eye for detail, Mark Twain sets the scene: this sleepy little town with its ramshackle houses and its loafers sitting around whittling and chewing tobacco. They amuse themselves by bad mouthing one another, setting up dog fights, and tying cans to the tails of dogs. Into this unrelievedly dreary scene Twain brings the drunken Boggs, who differs from the loafers already described only in his alcoholic belligerence. Boggs, however, commits a tactical error by attacking a gentleman whom Huck describes in the following sentence: "By-and-by a proud-looking man about fifty-five—and he was a heap the best-dressed man in that town, too— steps out of the store, and the crowd drops back on each side to let him come." Although Colonel Sherburn gives Boggs ample warning, when the time comes, Sherburn shoots him down in cold blood, before the eyes of Boggs' daughter. Sherburn further demonstrates his contempt for the townspeople by throwing his pistol on the ground and walking away. The scornful portrait of the town continues as the crowd jostles for a chance to see poor Boggs lying dead in the drugstore. As they adjourn to the street to watch the re-enactment of the shooting, it is evident that the affair has been essentially only an idle amusement, that there is no genuine concern for Boggs or his daughter. The decision to lynch Sherburn can thus be seen as just another diversion rather than the angry reaction of an outraged crowd.

The killing of Boggs is another instance of action in the novel taken directly from life and unified for furthering the development of the novel. On January 24, 1845, William Owsley shot an Uncle Sam Smarr in Hannibal, Missouri, when Clemens was still a boy. Apparently, Clemens did not witness the murder but he did see the murderer confront the mob. It is interesting that for a time, Colonel Sherburn becomes the central character of the novel and the narrative reaches over to his point of view, while Huck evaporates into nothingness.

We later learn that the name of this eroding town is Bricksville. It takes little imagination to see that the shabby condition of the town is a reflection of a deeper decay—that of the spirit of the citizenry, who lead wasteful and neglectful lives.

CHAPTER 22

Why the Lynching Failed

Summary

The aroused crowd charges to Colonel Sherburn's house, filling his front yard and tearing down his picket fence, but they quiet down when Sherburn steps onto his porch roof holding a gun. Sherburn proceeds to read off mankind in general, "Southern" mankind in particular, and especially this crowd. At the end of his tirade he braces his gun across his left arm and cocks it, at which point the crowd disappears.

In an abrupt shift, Huck leaves the scene and sneaks into the circus, where he has a marvelous time watching the performance. He is especially captivated by one trick-rider who pretends to be a drunken member of the audience. Huck thinks that the ring master has been completely fooled by one of his own men. After the circus, the duke's and king's show barely meets expenses. The duke then devises a new show that he says will make money—at the bottom of the playbill he has printed: "LADIES AND CHILDREN NOT ADMITTED."

Commentary

The Boggs-Sherburn incident is regarded as one of the most striking incidents in all of Twain's work, and rightly so. Sherburn's speech is considered one of the clearest statements of Twain's view of "the damned human race." As usual, Huck presents the scene without comment.

At the circus we see the extent of Huck's innocence. He accepts all the tawdry decorations of the circus as genuine, speculating that the women's clothes and "diamonds" must have cost millions of dollars. He is thoroughly taken in by the drunk act, one of the commonest acts in circuses of the period. The social criticism continues to the end of the chapter as the duke paints his come-on poster and observes: "If that line don't fetch them, I don't know Arkansaw!"

CHAPTER 23

The Orneriness of Kings

Summary

The next day the duke and the king rig up the performance for "The King's Cameleopard." As the duke has predicted, when the curtain goes up the house is full. After the duke makes a little curtain speech about his colleague, the king comes on naked, his body painted in an assortment of colors. He capers and cavorts around for a while as the audience roars with laughter. The curtain falls and the duke indicates the performance is over. The spectators are outraged when they realize they have been taken, but one suggests that unless they lure everybody else into attending the next night they will be laughed at as fools. The second night the whole thing is re-enacted with similar results. The third night, however, as Huck and the duke are collecting admissions at the door, Huck notices that the audience is concealing such things as rotten eggs, decayed fruit, and dead cats. As soon as the hall is filled the duke tells Huck it is time to leave, and quickly. Huck is a bit surprised to find the king already at the raft ahead of them, and they hastily shove off down the river. At this point Huck realizes that this was all part of the duke's plan. The duke and the king celebrate their dramatic success ($465 in three nights) by getting drunk, and Jim asks Huck if royalty always behaves this way. Huck gives Jim a rather confused history lecture to illustrate the way kings carry on, concluding that in comparison their king is not too bad.

At daybreak Huck wakens to hear Jim mourning for his family whom he misses terribly. In the conversation that follows, Jim tells Huck of the time he had punished his little daughter for not closing the door when he had told her to, only to realize a few minutes later that she was stone deaf as a result of scarlet fever and had been unable to hear his order. Jim says that he'll never forgive himself for hitting her.

Commentary

The success of "The King's Cameleopard" illustrates the psychology of the rural townsfolk and the ease with which an experienced confidence man like the duke can hoodwink them. The duke anticipates that the spectators' fear of being made to look foolish will prevent them from taking revenge before he has time to get out of town. Huck, with his usual moral neutrality, assists the duke and the king.

By contrast Jim's predicament directly involves Huck in an ethical situation. It is clear that Huck, like us, is moved by Jim's personal tragedy, but his natural sympathies conflict with the myths of the slave-holding society that has molded so much of his outlook. In the consistent pattern of his relationship with Jim, Huck's sense of humanity triumphs over society's teachings. The conflict, and the way in which Huck deals with it, is summarized when Huck says "I do believe he cared just as much for his people as white folks does for their'n. It don't seem natural but I reckon it's so."

CHAPTER 24

The King Turns Parson

Summary

The next day Jim complains about having to be tied up everytime he is left alone, so the duke dresses him in theatrical robes, paints his face blue, then writes out a sign: "Sick Arab—but harmless when not out of his head." Everyone agrees that this will scare off any curious strangers. The duke and the king then try to work out their next campaign and agree that the next village is too close to the previous one to run the "Cameleopard" again safely. The king then decides to dress up in the store clothes he bought and explore the town, taking along Huck as his servant. On shore, they encounter a young man waiting for the steamboat and the king offers him a ride in the canoe. On the way the young man tells them about the death the previous night of Peter Wilks, a well-to-do tanner in the village. The king learns that Wilks' heirs are two brothers, who have been in England, and three nieces, who are in the village. The brothers, one of whom is deaf and dumb, are expected to return any day. The king pumps the young man for more information about the Wilks family and their friends, then puts him on the steamboat for New Orleans. The king, duke, and Huck paddle upstream, where they board another steamboat so that they can arrive in the village as if from farther up river. The king presents himself as the elder of Peter Wilks' brothers, who is a minister, and the duke takes the part of the brother who is deaf and dumb. Huck goes along with them as a body servant. To Huck's amazement, the townspeople accept the imposters without question.

Commentary

This chapter is almost a textbook case for confidence men. We see the king setting out for the village without the remotest idea of how he is going to turn a buck. When he encounters the young man who babbles out information about the Wilks family, he immediately sizes up the situation and sets in motion a scheme whereby he and the duke can get their hands on the Wilks' money. The manner in which he pumps information from the young man, and his skilful use of what he finds out, might be taken as a model for any confidence man in training.

Through most of this development, Huck remains in the background, morally neutral, but the baldness and shamelessness of the performance exact a significant outburst from him at the end of the chapter: "Well if ever I struck anything like it, I'm a nigger. It was enough to make a body ashamed of the human race." This is the first break in Huck's moral neutrality since the duke and the king joined them. It sets the stage for Huck's ethical decision at the end of the Wilks episode.

The form in which Huck chooses to express his dismay is also significant. Despite the special quality of his relationship with Jim, Huck, like all the other whites he knows, regards Negroes in general as something less than human. Equating himself with a "nigger" is the most unlikely comparison he can think of.

CHAPTER 25

All Full of Tears and Flapdoodle

Summary

With Huck in attendance the scoundrels work themselves quickly into the confidence of the Wilks girls. Mary Jane, the eldest niece, gives them Peter Wilks' last letter, which tells his brothers that he has hidden six thousand dollars in the cellar. The imposters go downstairs to count the money, and discover the amount is less than had been announced. They make up the difference from their own cash to avoid difficulties and to make a good impression. The king carries his end of the show rather too broadly and is accused of being a fraud by the highly educated Dr. Robinson, who arrives toward the end of the chapter. However, the town has gone so far toward accepting the king and the duke as the true Harvey and William Wilks from England that they hoot the doctor down. The Wilks girls show their faith by giving the money to the king, and the doctor washes his hands of the whole affair.

Commentary

Twain once more presents a portrait of the gullibility of what he refers to in another work as the "damned human race." In *Huckleberry Finn*, as in so many of his works, he is concerned with the vagaries of man, holding them up to ridicule. Twain shows us man's inability to see and cope with the truth, and the extent to which man can be lied to. Twain portrays this in the sections in which Huck reacts negatively to religion, in the revival scene in which the king manages to fleece the people with the story about being a missionary to pirates, and in the incident of "The King's Cameleopard." Man's inclination, as Twain sees it, is to fasten on the nearest (*not* the most reasonable) fancy and cling to it despite all subsequent evidence to the contrary. Thus we can with Huck, and presumably his author, be "ashamed of the human race."

CHAPTER 26

I Steal the King's Plunder

Summary

The three girls provide quarters for their "uncles" and Huck, with Mary Jane giving up her own room to the king. After dinner, during which the duke and the king "butter up" their victims, Huck finds himself cornered by Joanna, the harelipped sister, who questions him about life in England. As Joanna later puts it, Huck (of course inventing as he goes along) tells her some "stretchers." When she has him swear to the truth on what Huck slyly notices is a dictionary, her expressed reservations about his honesty are overheard by her sisters, Mary Jane and Susan. The two sisters reprimand Joanna for picking on poor Huck who is away from his home in England, and finally Joanna apologizes to Huck. At this point Huck is emotionally in shreds: he feels he can no longer simply stand by as he has done in the previous exploits of the king and the duke—and let the two con men fleece these lovely girls. He slips into the king's room to search for the money. When he hears the king and the duke coming, Huck hides behind Mary Jane's frocks and listens as the two frauds argue about their course of action. The duke, exhibiting a bit of conscience, is all for absconding that night with the money they have, but the king convinces him that they should stick around to sell the house and property. Huck sees where they hide the money, and after they leave he takes it to his cubby in the garret.

Commentary

Huck's decision to help the Wilks girls may at first seem inconsistent with the morally neutral position he has taken in all the previous episodes in the towns along the river. It should be noted, however, that Huck refuses to take sides only when the confrontation is between what society considers good and evil. Huck is, after all, an outcast himself and has ample reasons for rejecting society's code of morality. He does have a strong personal sense of ethics that comes to the fore in his relationships with people for whom he can develop affection. This sense of ethics is the ultimate controlling force in his crucial decisions about Jim; it now impels him to play an active role in the destiny of the Wilks girls. Its influence can also be seen in his attempt to help the cutthroats on the wreck of the *Walter Scott* (because the Widow Douglas would have approved his action) and in his expression of regret at being the unwitting instrument in setting off the fight between the Shepherdsons and Grangerfords, who had been kind to him. In this light we can see that Huck's choice is completely in character.

CHAPTER 27

Dead Peter has His Gold

Summary

Having taken the money from the place where the duke and the king have hidden it, Huck stealthily places it in the coffin with the body of Peter Wilks. In the morning the funeral begins, and Peter Wilks is buried with all due ceremony. The con men then proceed with their plan to sell the house, the land, and the slaves, and promise to take the three girls to England with them—which delights the girls. Everybody is happy until the slaves are to be sold: the king sells the two sons upriver to Memphis, and their mother down river to New Orleans. The girls are considerably disturbed by this, but the slaves are taken away. Huck stands back knowing that he can expose the fraud by dropping a letter as he and the con men leave. The next day, just before the auction to sell the house and the property, the king discovers that the money is missing. He and the duke question Huck who manages to transfer blame to the slaves; the duke quarrels with the king, as Huck slips away congratulating himself for having successfully blamed the slaves who are by now with their new masters where they cannot be reached.

Commentary

Huck's description of the funeral is another of Twain's satiric commentaries on middle-class rituals and its dependence on shabby elegance.

We should note Twain's use, in the dialogue between the king and the duke, of the motif of "when thieves fall out." Under the impact of the loss of the money, the duke and the king begin quarreling between themselves about who is to blame for the loss.

CHAPTER 28

Overreaching Don't Pay

Summary

Huck finds Mary Jane crying and she tells him how sad she is at the break-up of the slave family. Huck, trying to comfort her, blurts out that she will soon have the slaves back. He begs her to do what he says, telling her as much of the story as she needs to know. Mary Jane agrees to visit a friend for a few days because, as Huck points out, she would be unable to act naturally before her "uncles." Huck tells Susan and Joanna that Mary Jane has gone to nurse a sick friend, and they all go out to watch the conduct of the auction. The clever king has sold nearly everything, when suddenly a crowd comes from the steamboat landing bringing with them *another* pair of brothers of old Peter Wilks.

Commentary

For a person who lies as much as he does, poor Huck can be un-professional about it at times. He is continually getting his stories muddled and almost getting caught. In this instance, he confuses the name of the person who is sick, he twists up the illness, and, most significantly, he informs Mary Jane that it is all a lie. On the basis of this evidence and other general evidence of Huck's clumsiness at lying, we must conclude that Huck is not basically untruthful. In this narrative, Huck must rather be seen as using his lies as a form of protection. He does not have a clearly defined identity and further covers his identity by his lies.

Note also that Huck again mentions his model, Tom Sawyer, in ref-erence to the story he makes up, reckoning that "Tom Sawyer couldn't a done it no neater himself. Of course, he would a throwed more style into it, but I can't do that very handy, not being brung up to it." Tom would indeed have given the story more style, but by the time he had finished the whole cause would have been lost. The essence of Huck's plans is that, lacking style, they are clean, simple, take maximum account of human frailties, and are almost guaranteed to work despite any problems that might arise.

CHAPTER 29

I Light Out in the Storm

Summary

In this chapter, the king and the duke, along with the two newcomers, are subjected to a series of tests aimed at determining who are the real brothers of Peter Wilks. Huck recognizes from the first that the English accent of one of the new arrivals is infinitely superior to that of the king, but the townspeople are committed to their original position and are loath to accept or even intelligently consider the newcomers. They do accept a series of tests, based in part on the testimony of a man named Hines who had seen the king and Huck pumping the young man on his way to New Orleans. The tests are pushed along by Dr. Robinson with the aid of the laywer, Levi Bell, but at each step it is apparent that the tests would be dropped except for their insistence. Although the king fails each test, he manages to come up with an explanation which the people in general accept. The final test proposed by the new Harvey Wilks involves a tattoo mark on the deceased Peter Wilks' breast. The men who had handled the body do not remember any tattoo, so the crowd, with Huck, the king, and the duke under restraint, head for the graveyard. During the confusion which follows the discovery of the bag of gold Huck had put in the coffin, Huck escapes to the raft and pushes off, thinking that he and Jim are now free of the king and the duke. However, in just minutes, the king and the duke catch them, rowing a skiff for their lives!

Commentary

This chapter is a perfect example of the storyteller's art. Mark Twain develops the series of tests, ending each one ambiguously, thereby delaying the climax of this episode. When that climax finally comes with the discovery of the gold in the coffin, the reader has the satisfaction of having been held in suspense despite knowing the gold would be found. The timing that Mark Twain shows in this chapter is one of the reasons why we call him a master storyteller.

One of the most important minor figures in the Wilks episode is Dr. Robinson, who should be noted as one of the few people whom Huck respects. Dr. Robinson has recognized that Huck is not a professional confidence man like the king and the duke, and Dr. Robinson's knowledge of man has made him a cynic. There is little doubt that he reflects Twain's own views.

CHAPTER 30

The Gold Saves the Thieves

Summary

Huck convinces the king and the duke that he and Jim were not running out on them. The two men then begin to quarrel about how the money got into the coffin. Each suspects the other, but the king confesses when the duke starts to choke him. Then they get drunk together and make up. After they fall asleep Huck tells Jim about their adventures on land.

Commentary

The main point in this chapter is the old cliche that "there's no honor among thieves." We see the king and the duke arguing about who was trying to hide the money. Each assumes that the other was trying to do him in because each knows that this was his own intention. And this is most obvious in the duke's forcing the king to "admit" that he was the one who hid the money in the coffin. Here all the subtleties of the confidence game are laid aside, and the duke resorts to brute force to get his point across. The squabbling between the two crooks is a relief to Huck, for it prevents them from questioning him too closely.

CHAPTER 31

You Can't Pray A Lie

Summary

The duke and the king try several of their schemes in the various towns they hit, but nothing is successful and they become more and more morose as their money runs out. Finally the king, making use of the handbill the duke had printed up, sells Jim to a Silas Phelps for forty dollars as his share of the two hundred dollar "reward." He does this without consulting the duke or Huck, and then gets drunk and loses the money. When Huck finds out what has happened he wrestles with his conscience on the question of whether to help Jim escape or to let Miss Watson know where he is. At first he decides that he should turn Jim in. He writes a note to Miss Watson, but then remembers how good Jim has been to him and how close they have been. Finally he tears up the note, pronouncing judgment on himself: "All right, then, I'll *go* to hell." He sets out for the Phelps farm but runs into the duke, to whom he tells a cock-and-bull story about the location of the raft. Huck does not let on that he knows where Jim is and pretends to believe the duke when he tells Huck that Jim is on a farm forty miles away. The duke is obviously trying to get rid of Huck, who he thinks may inform on him, so Huck sets out in what seems to be the wrong direction. As soon as the duke is out of sight, Huck doubles back to the farm of Silas Phelps.

Commentary

It is in this chapter that Huck most fully comes to grips with his moral dilemma. As has been said before, Huck is a child of the slave-holding Mississippi Valley, and as such he believes slave-holding to be right. He has been taught that anyone who attempts to free a slave is an agent of, almost literally, the devil. Nevertheless, his personal sense of ethics (see "Commentary," Chapter 26) determines his ultimate decision. Notice that he accepts society's judgment that what he is doing is wrong, but his solution is to brand himself completely as an outcast. If he is going to hell anyway, there is no point in trying to reform. He puts it this way: "I shoved the whole thing out of my head, and said I would take up wickedness again, which was in my line, being brung up to it, and the other warn't . . . as long as I was in, and in for good, I might as well go the whole hog." As we will see in the next chapter, Huck's conversion affects only his relationship with Jim; it does not influence his attitudes about Negroes in general.

Chapter 32

I Have A New Name

Summary

When Huck comes to the Phelps farm, he is pinned down by several dogs, as he had been earlier at the Grangerfords. The dogs are called off by a woman who greets him as if she had been expecting him. Huck, responding almost without thinking, assumes the role of "Cousin Tom," although he has no idea who Tom is. He guesses that he would be expected to have come down river on a steamboat, so when "Aunt Sally" asks what kept him he tells her that they blew out a cylinder head on the boat. She responds: "Good gracious! Anybody hurt?" He answers: "No'm. Killed a nigger." She rattles on until Silas Phelps comes in, and in joking with her husband, reveals that the cousin she has been expecting is Tom Sawyer. Greatly relieved, Huck spends the next few hours telling them all sorts of stories about the Sawyer family. Then he hears a steamboat on the river and, concerned that Tom will show up before he can talk to him, invents an excuse for walking down the road where he hopes to intercept Tom.

Commentary

Huck's response to Aunt Sally's question about the "accident" is indicative of Huck's attitude toward slaves in general. Neither for Aunt Sally Phelps, who is a good-hearted soul, nor for Huck himself, are Negroes "anybody" or as Aunt Sally puts it, "people." The death of a slave does not represent the loss of a human being to these two residents of the pre-Civil War Mississippi Valley.

The description of the Phelps farm is modelled on the farm of Sam Clemens' Uncle John Quarles. This farm is described at some length in Mark Twain's *Autobiography*. Quarles' farm was located near Hannibal, and according to Twain's account, he was often a guest at his Uncle John's. Twain later used the Quarles' farm in *Tom Sawyer, Detective*, in which Aunt Sally and Uncle Silas are important characters and Huck is again the narrator.

CHAPTER 33

The Pitiful Ending Of Royalty

Summary

Huck sets out toward town and meets Tom on the way. Tom first thinks that Huck is a ghost, but Huck quickly convinces him that it was all an adventure. Then Huck tells Tom about Jim. Tom starts to say something, but thinks better of it, and tells Huck he will help steal Jim from the Phelpses. Huck is very surprised that Tom would cooperate in freeing a slave. Huck returns to the Phelps house first, and when Tom arrives about an hour later he represents himself as a total stranger. Tom proceeds to invent a long story about himself, but then makes the mistake of kissing Aunt Sally on the mouth, whereupon she chastises him unmercifully. Tom gets himself out of the jam by saying that he is really Sid Sawyer, his older brother, who has talked Aunt Polly into letting him come too. At dinner one of the Phelps boys asks if he and Tom and Sid can go to the show in town, which Huck realizes is the duke's and the king's "Royal Nonesuch." Uncle Silas says that the runaway slave has told him what kind of a show it is, and the townspeople are ready to drive the "owdacious loafers" out of town. Tom and Huck plead fatigue and go off to their room, but slip out immediately because Huck wants to run into town to warn the king and the duke. On the road they see a crowd of people carrying torches and in their midst on a rail, two figures covered with tar and feathers. Even though he knows what kind of men they are, Huck feels sorry for the duke and the king, "Human beings can be awful cruel to one another."

Commentary

It should first be noted that Tom starts to tell Huck something about Jim and then lets it drop; this is another detail the author has planted (see "Commentary," Chapter 9) to set the stage for the final resolution at the end of the book.

This chapter also provides further evidence of Huck's essential humanity. Just as he had tried to help the cutthroats on the *Walter Scott*, he tries to warn the scoundrels who have used him and betrayed Jim; when it is evident that he is too late, he feels sorry for them and even a little to blame for their predicament, although he knows he did the best he could. As Huck puts it, "that's always the way; it don't make no difference whether you do right or wrong, a person's conscience ain't got no sense, and just goes for him anyway."

CHAPTER 34

We Cheer Up Jim

Summary

Huck and Tom attempt to find out where Jim is being kept, and Tom notices that food is being carried into a shack on the back of the farm. They are sure that this is where Jim is. When Huck devises a plan to free Jim, Tom concedes that it would work but argues that it is too simple, that there is "nothing to it." Then Tom himself comes up with a plan. Huck goes along with it because it has "style," even though it is more dangerous and will take longer. Huck doesn't tell us what the plan is, because, as he says, "I knowed it wouldn't stay the way it was." They examine the cabin which, as Huck points out, has a window big enough for Jim to crawl out of if they wrench off a board, but Tom decides that they should dig Jim out, which will take at least a week. The next day they trick the slave who feeds Jim into letting them in to see him, and they let Jim know that they are planning to free him.

Commentary

Here we see Huck coming again under the influence of Tom Sawyer, as he was in the early chapters having to do with the "pirate gang." From this point on, Huck is in constant conflict, having to choose between the "stylish" things that Tom wants to do and his own common sense. In these conflicts, Tom's "style" always wins over common sense.

CHAPTER 35

Dark, Deep-laid Plans

Summary

Having located Jim, Tom and Huck begin to work on the details of getting him out. Jim's situation is very simple. He is chained to the leg of a bed, and all he has to do is lift the bed and remove the chain. The old shack he is in couldn't hold anyone who wanted to get out of it. Tom, however, will have nothing to do with anything easy. As he puts it, "You got to invent *all* the difficulties." And so Tom plans to have Jim saw through the leg of the bed rather than just lift it up (he does reject the idea of having Jim cut off his own leg), and to have Jim make a rope ladder. He speculates on digging a moat for Jim to stumble into, and he plans to have Jim write a journal or at least make marks on a shirt. They have to steal plates for Jim to mark messages on, for that is the way it is done in the romantic novels, even though Jim is fed from a pan rather than a plate. Then they have to get the most difficult kinds of tools to use rather than picks and hoes that are lying in the very shack in which Jim is imprisoned. At the end of the debate Tom is thoroughly in command, and he sends Huck to steal knives to use for digging.

Commentary

As in the earlier chapters on the "pirate gang," we can see here Mark Twain's dislike for the romantic novel; among the writers he most despised were Scott and Dumas. Tom is very much under the influence of writers of this kind, and all his plans for getting Jim out are chuckle-headed variations on events from their novels, especially from Dumas' *The Count of Monte Cristo*. Huck continually interposes common-sense objections, so Tom ultimately throws up his hands at ever trying to teach Huck how to plan with "style" and simply takes over total direction.

CHAPTER 36

Trying To Help Jim

Summary

With Tom in thorough control, the "rescue" begins as soon as the rest of the family is asleep. Tom quickly realizes that digging with case knives is going to take too long, but he adjusts to the situation by pretending that picks and shovels are case knives. Huck adjusts to the make-believe by giving Tom a pick every time he asks for a case knife. The second night they get through to Jim and find him in good condition. Uncle Silas and Aunt Sally have been coming down and praying with him almost every day, making sure he is comfortable and getting plenty to eat. Jim, like Huck, can't see any sense in Tom's plan when it is explained to him, but he goes along with it because Tom and Huck are "white folks" and Jim assumes that they know better than he does. Tom is thrilled with the whole project and talks about continuing it the rest of their lives, passing Jim as an inheritance to their children. The chapter ends with Tom again playing on the superstitious fears of Jim's keeper, Nat, so that later he can smuggle in a rope ladder in a "witch pie."

Commentary

Tom's absurd distortions have both comic and painful aspects. Not only does he carry on the pretense by calling the picks and shovels "case knives," but at the end of the first night, when he is too worn out from digging to climb the lightning rod, he accepts Huck's suggestion that he use the house stairs and "let on it's a lightning rod." In his insistence on making an adventurous game of everything he does, Tom uses Jim, the slave, Nat, and even Huck simply as pawns, and Jim's freedom is cruelly delayed.

CHAPTER 37

Jim Gets His Witch-Pie

Summary

Jim's "saviours" find themselves in a predicament because Aunt Sally has begun to look for various things the boys have stolen for Jim. At first she blames Uncle Silas who good-naturedly accepts responsibility. Tom and Huck then fluster Aunt Sally by secretly putting in and taking away spoons as she counts them until the poor woman no longer trusts her own ability to count. They then follow the same routine with sheets and candlesticks.

Huck and Tom borrow Silas' warming-pan in order to bake their pie. After a number of failures, a crusted pie containing the rope ladder for Jim's escape is finally made and delivered to Jim. Nat, the Phelps' servant, turns his back as requested, happy that the hungry witches will now be fed and will no longer bother him.

Commentary

The comic aspects of Tom's wild schemes are counterbalanced by our awareness of the suffering they cause everybody else, including Aunt Sally and Uncle Silas. Tom shamelessly uses them as objects of sport, confusing them over the things he and Huck have stolen in order to cover their tracks and avoid detection. Tom, in fact, gives no thought to the consequences of his actions and simply finds his "fun" wherever he can. When we consider the feelings of Aunt Sally and Uncle Silas, we realize that Tom has put them through a painful experience.

CHAPTER 38

Here A Captive Heart Busted

Summary

Tom believes every prisoner must scribble an inscription on his prison wall before breaking out. Tom makes up four inscriptions, the first of which is: "Here a captive heart busted." Tom also insists that Jim have a coat-of-arms, which, along with all four suggested inscriptions, must be scratched on a grindstone.

Tom also suggests a rattlesnake as a pet for Jim and a flower to be watered with Jim's tears. Jim is afraid the flower will die because he hardly ever cries.

Commentary

Here, again, Twain pokes fun at royalty and the waste of human energy over vain and snobbish preoccupations, such as a coat-of-arms. Twain also satirizes the sentimental romance with the references to the inscriptions and the tear-watered flower.

CHAPTER 39

Tom Writes Nonnamous Letters

Summary

Tom and Huck proceed to catch rats, snakes, and spiders, which they plan to put in Jim's cabin to fit Tom's conception of the dungeons he has read about. Unfortunately, most of these creatures get loose in the house, and greatly upset Aunt Sally. Huck and Tom are whipped several times, but this does not deter them. They collect another load of assorted vermin and loose them on poor Jim, whose good-natured complaints are unavailing. Meanwhile Uncle Silas decides to advertise about Jim in the St. Louis papers, since he has had no answer to his letters to the nonexistent plantation below New Orleans. Huck realizes that they have to free Jim soon, and Tom says it is time to send the "nonnamous" letters. The first turns out to be a vague warning to the family, and the second is a detailed account of the plans of a gang of cutthroats to steal "the runaway nigger." Both are signed, "Unknown Friend."

Commentary

The Phelps farm episode is the funniest in the book, and this chapter is the comic climax. The reservations we may have felt in the preceding chapters are overwhelmed by the absurd results of Tom's shenanigans. The picture of this sober frontier household beset by snakes, rats, spiders, and frogs is one that few readers will ever forget. Tom, of course, gives no thought to the consequences of his actions. As we shall see in the next chapter, farm folk living on this eastern edge of the frontier did not take lightly the threat of any kind of raid. This is understandable when we remember that in those times bands of desperadoes like the James and Younger gangs and Quantrill's Raiders were moving through Arkansas, the Oklahoma Territory, and Kansas.

CHAPTER 40

A Mixed-Up and Splendid Rescue

Summary

Tom and Huck are ready to begin the final phase of the escape. Tom sends Huck down to the cellar to get some butter while he goes to the shed to make a straw dummy of Jim, planning that the three of them will leave as soon as Huck returns. Aunt Sally discovers Huck in the cellar and brings him upstairs, where he finds fifteen farmers with guns waiting to help Silas Phelps defend himself against the gang of cutthroats they expect at midnight. As soon as Aunt Sally sends him to bed, he slides down the lightning rod and joins Tom and Jim. Some of the farmers come into the cabin before the boys can get out, but they duck out through the hole they have dug. Tom's breeches catch on a rail splinter, and the noise alerts the farmers who chase them with dogs and guns. The fugitives make it to the raft but discover that Tom has been shot in the leg. Tom is thrilled at having been wounded, but Jim and Huck insist that he has to have a doctor. After promising to follow Tom's complicated instructions, Huck jumps in the canoe and sets out for town.

Commentary

In this chapter we see Huck and Jim facing the consequences of Tom's plan, at best a harebrained scheme and at worst downright dangerous. In order to succeed, the plan has to be reinforced by the practical sense of Jim and Huck which tempers Tom's "style." Jim loses his freedom but displays a humanity and compassion that sharply contrasts with Tom's attitudes.

For this fleeting moment in the last chapters, Huck and Jim become their former selves. It must be remarked that only when they are far from the farm does this change occur. The return to the river has made Huck instantly resourceful. He can move, and he can move swiftly. Jim becomes the tender and humane person who had stood watch for Huck time and again. It is the environs of the river that charge these two with real life.

CHAPTER 41

Must A' Been Sperits

Summary

Huck finds the doctor and tells him a story of his own devising, but the doctor is clearly suspicious. He insists on going to the island by himself, and Huck goes to sleep on shore. In the morning Huck runs into Uncle Silas, who takes him back to the farm. The farm is filled with visitors, all talking about the strange things they have found in the shack where Jim was kept prisoner. Everyone agrees that such strange goings-on must have been the work of spirits. While everyone is still looking for "Sid" and the runaway slave, Aunt Sally brings Huck back into his room. Huck feels that he cannot repay her kindness by sneaking out again, so despite his uneasiness about Tom, he stays in the house.

Commentary

Twain once more demonstrates how easily frontier folk took to the supernatural to explain events they were unable to understand. Aunt Sally's statement that "sperits" must have been at work because otherwise the dogs would have barked is readily accepted by her friends.

CHAPTER 42

Why They Didn't Hang Jim

Summary

In the morning Uncle Silas gives Aunt Sally a letter from Tom's Aunt Polly in St. Petersburg. Before she can open it, the unconscious Tom is brought in on a mattress followed by the doctor and Jim, with his hands tied behind him. The doctor and the elder Phelpses go off to minister to Tom, and the remaining farmers angrily haul Jim off. They cuff and abuse him and threaten to hang him, but they cool off a little when they realize they would have to pay his owner. They then load him down with chains and throw him in the cabin. When the doctor comes back he tells the crowd to treat Jim more kindly because it was Jim who helped him save Tom's life, even though he could have gotten away if he had chosen to. Huck is relieved when the farmers agree to stop cussing and cuffing Jim, although they make no move to remove the chains.

Tom is better the next morning, and when Huck and Aunt Sally go in to see him, Tom babbles out the whole story thinking that Jim has succeeded in getting away. When Aunt Sally tells him that Jim is chained in the shack, Tom announces that Jim had been freed by Miss Watson in her will. At this point Aunt Polly appears in the doorway. She of course identifies Tom Sawyer and Huck Finn, explaining that she had come herself because she had gotten no answers to her letters inquiring about Sally's references to Sid. As it turns out, Tom had intercepted all the letters but the last.

Commentary

Except for a few loose ends, this chapter concludes the story of Huckleberry Finn. With the exposure of Tom and Huck, and the freeing of Jim, the whole Phelps farm fantasy is resolved and the action is ended.

Note than once more Twain provides a role for the reasonable man, in this case the doctor, whose timely arrival prevents the farmers from further abusing and perhaps injuring Jim.

Aunt Polly's arrival, which some critics have described as a *deux ex machina*, is in fact satisfactorily explained by the series of intercepted letters.

CHAPTER 43

Nothing More To Write

Summary

As soon as they are alone Huck asks Tom what he planned to do had the escape succeeded entirely. Tom says that he intended to pursue the adventure down to the mouth of the river, then he planned to tell Jim he was free, and bring him back up in a steamboat in style. Huck comments that "it was about as well the way it was." Jim is released and brought to the house, where Aunt Sally makes a big fuss over him. Tom gives Jim forty dollars to make up for all the trouble he caused him and then says they should all go to the Oklahoma Territory to seek more adventures. When Huck says he is sure Pap has taken all his money, Jim then reveals that the dead man he and Huck had seen in the floating house much earlier was Pap. As the book ends, Huck observes that he had better head out to the Territory ahead of the others because Aunt Sally is going to adopt him and "sivilize" him. "I can't stand it. I been there before. *The End, Huck Finn.*"

Commentary

This final chapter is something of an epilogue, in which the remaining loose ends are tied up. The last few lines have been the subject of much critical commentary. Perhaps it is enough for us to observe that in the past Huck has often failed to carry out his resolutions. Whether he will do so this time is something for each reader to decide for himself.

Characters

Methods of Analyzing Characters

1. Describing the Characters

One effective way to begin an analysis of any character in a novel is to make a list of all the things the character says about himself, and then to make a list of those things that others say about him. Sometimes these references or allusions may not be complimentary; however, they are revealing. For example, Pap Finn is disliked by almost everyone in the book. The unkindest things are usually said about him. The overall testimony would support the view that Pap Finn is not a good man. Moreover, he does not pretend to be anything but the scoundrel that he is. Only at one point can we see his life as admirable, and that is when he takes Huck off to the shack with him. Pap Finn comes out of the pages as real, intense, and alive when we see him through his own eyes and the eyes of those around him.

2. Character Development

The process of character development in a novel can be traced in two ways. One way is to examine the character from the moment that he appears in the book—either by being referred to or as really present. Gradually we begin to form some opinion about this character as we learn more and more about him. Pap Finn may mean nothing to the reader at first. Gradually, or suddenly, he begins to form as a real man. Most characters come into a novel with some advantage. Since each is unknown, he received the benefit of any doubt. However, character development can be more than mere development in representation. It can also indicate change. Each of us changes by meeting other people or by undergoing certain experiences. Few people are the same as they were yesterday. The same development takes place in the novel. A rounded character, as E.M. Foster has so aptly explained in his *Aspects of the Novel*, is one that changes. A flat character does not. Huck is absolutely amazed that Tom Sawyer will help Jim to escape. For Tom, this is change, rapid change; it is surprise. However, we come to realize that there has been no grave psychological change in Tom. He knew all the time that Jim was already free. Yet even here we have character development. Tom has further defined his own potentialities. We know more now of his willingness to be amused than we did before. The short story usually involves one psychological change whereby we realize that one person or more will never again be the same. Character development in a novel can involve a number of such changes.

3. Motivation

In actual life we are constantly plagued by the problem of motive. It is usually impossible to know the motivation of another person. The wise man reserves judgment in these things because he realizes that he does not know even his own motivation. In a novel we can toy with motivations as we read. In this way, we can come to see how wrong are our judgments of motivation. We take Judge Thatcher to be a good man for reasons already alluded to in discussing character development. When he takes all of Huck's gold from him for one dollar, we do not doubt the motivation of the judge, even though no immediate explanation of the transaction is offered. The reader is asked to infer the motivation of the judge in setting up a technical barrier to Pap's getting Huck's gold. If the judge should cheat Huck, we would be hard pressed to understand his motivation and perhaps we would need another novel to explain what made him do it. Such behavior would be out of keeping with the general tone of the novel. Toward the end of the novel, we learn that Huck still has his money in good hands. Although all the evidence pointed to the murder of Huck by some mysterious stranger, Pap cannot get the money from the judge. In keeping with the kind of person we now know the judge to be, the author and the reader realize that the crafty judge will want much more proof of Huck's death than circumstantial evidence. We don't know if Pap ever tried to claim Huck's money because of the suspected murder, yet we can imagine the judge would never give it to him. A novel can do just so much. It cannot be all of life. We can know the "why" of a character's action only as it relates to the general theme or purpose of the novel.

It is precisely here that the novel can be defined as art and not as life. The novel extracts from life to be more than life. It give us an order and an understanding of life and a consistency in motivation for the moment. Things make sense in a novel, and there is time and space to explain only just so much. Loose ends may exist in life, but too many loose ends can ruin a novel. This statement is not to say that all of a novel can be explained. The statement merely suggests that we can be satisfied with reasonable inferences or explanations when we do analyze a novel.

4. Theme and Character

To continue our discussion of analyzing characters, we move from motivation and art to theme. In a novel, a character can more easily take on meaning because the novel does not range as far as life. We do not mean to say that a character must represent some theme or meaning of life; nevertheless, he usually does. In some usages, a flat character may be allegorical or ideal. No doubt Miss Watson represents a trait in some women who feel compelled to reform others. She may also represent the thematic character whose entire morality is drawn only from the Bible. However, it is good to realize that such interpretations of Miss Watson may prevent us from seeing more about her. It is always a bad idea to put a thematic sign on a character so that he is not free. Sometimes an author must restrict his characters to develop a larger purpose in his novel. Some critic once said that Shakespeare had to kill Mercutio rather early in *Romeo and Juliet* because he was stealing the whole play. All in all, we can say that no character can be totally saddled with a theme to represent something. But on the other hand, art usually does reveal a representation that makes life more clear to us. A novel has a purpose and each character supports this purpose. If Pap Finn comes as a man at odds with his society, he merely prefigures Huck who is more decently and more grandly ready to escape his society. If Miss Watson needs to reform Huck, it may urge him to seek escape from reform. Where there is conflict, and the novel, like drama, involves conflict, there are opposites. The human faculty to create allegory out of opposites can make good and evil leap from the page. This thematic representation has been true in English since Boewulf and Grendel.

5. Environment

No character can exist in a novel without some relationship to space. A character exists in a specific environment. The theory of the novel abounds in discussions concerning the influence of environment on characters. However critical, however absolute, or however ineffectual, the relationship varies from one novel or one view of life to another. The environment can produce effect in the demeanor of a character. His entire attitude or his behavior may vary with his location. If a person is at ease in one atmosphere, he may not be quick to act. In another, he may be just itching to make a move and the slightest event will give him immediate cause to act. We sometimes speak of such an event as an epiphany. Epiphany means no more than the sudden realization of some truth about the nature of the world or the nature of oneself. It can come out of any mood, but always occurs in a particular environment.

6. Relationships in the Novel

It is possible to write a novel about one man and his environment. Such novels are rare because a life of solitude is rare. People are defined, usually, by people. Each of us accumulates many traces of people we meet in life. Some are slight, some are profound. Our acquisition of mannerisms, however, does not define us as much as the experience of interacting with others. We change, often, because people make us change. We exercise virtue or vice when we meet others. We cannot begin to be sure of any virtue or vice until we see the response of man to man. What one character does to another provides a ready means of character analysis, but it must be tempered by our ideas of motivation and theme and environment. We use this method most because we judge the excellence of a novel by the credibility of the relationships of the characters.

Character Sketches

Huckleberry Finn

Huck Finn is one of America's best-loved fictional characters. Critically, he has been the subject of numerous studies and interpretations, many of them so unique as to make Huck unrecognizable.

Since Huck is the narrator of a book filled with humor, it is highly significant that we recognize that Huck himself has little sense of humor; in fact, he is almost totally literal minded. It is inconceivable to him that the drunk riding the horse at the circus is really a highly trained acrobat. For a while, he literally believes a genie can be made to appear by rubbing an old lamp.

Since Huck is so completely literal minded, he therefore makes a superb narrator in that he tells or reports everything he sees or hears with straightforward accuracy. He never exaggerates or embroiders on anything he narrates and, therefore, we can always trust Huck's account or narration of any event to be realistic.

Huck possesses most of the qualities which are necessary for life on the frontier. He is always practical and natural, exhibiting good common sense except in such rare episodes as the snake episode. Furthermore, Huck is extremely adaptable. He can learn to tolerate living with the Widow Douglas and then can quickly transform his ways to that of living in the wilderness, living on a raft, or living in the "so-called" elegance of the Grangerfords. Huck's adaptability, then, allows him to function well in different types of situations.

In order to protect himself, Huck constantly takes on new identities, which also serve to isolate him from the society around him. Thus, Huck is shrewd enough to be able to determine what motivates such people as the "bounty hunters," and then he is inventive enough to create a story which is so credible that he and Jim are left alone. But Huck often lies poorly, particularly when he is confounded by the circumstances that impel him to lie. Thus the stories he makes up on the river to protect both himself and Jim are quite believable, while the lies he tells in the Wilks household and on the Phelps farm are transparent and inconsistent. Huck, in short, functions very well in uncomplicated situations.

Huck is also a person who responds sympathetically to other human beings. He tries to save the cutthroats on the *Walter Scott*; he saves the king and the duke from a posse and later even feels sorry for them when they are tarred and feathered; and he responds deeply to the plight of the Wilks girls. This is the same quality which allows him to appreciate and love Jim.

Huck's sympathy for other human beings, his shrewdness and ingenuity, his basic intelligence, his good common sense and his basic practicality—these are among the qualities which make Huck Finn one of the great characters in American fiction.

Jim

Except for Huck himself, the most clearly distinguishable major character is Jim. At every point in the story there are Negro slaves attending the whites, but with the exception of Jim all the slaves are really part of the general background. This position results obviously from Huck's role as narrator, and it reflects his attitude toward Negroes in general. Jim, however, receives much fuller treatment because of the partnership begun on Jackson's Island. As he emerges in the narrative Jim is clearly drawn.

Jim is generous, shrewd, superstitious, practical, and experienced in the ways of the Mississippi Valley. However, we should also note that Twain has Jim depend for judgment on the nearest white man whenever he can, and that abstractions like languages are simply more than he can handle by himself.

Further, Jim has no conception of money value in any practical terms, as we see in the last chapter. He is not only satisfied with the forty dollars Tom gives him, but is actually happy with it and regards himself as rich. As we see him at the end of the narrative he seems perfectly willing to let Tom and Huck lead and protect him. Raised as a slave, Jim has not been trained to use his own judgment; he has been trained to look to and depend on the masters for guidance.

In no way should a discussion of Jim's limitations be allowed to detract from his strengths. He possesses many practical abilities. He rigs the raft; he is the guide on the journey down the river from St. Petersburg (Hannibal) to below Cairo; he is the one who nurses Tom when he is wounded. Indeed, Jim and Huck, the practical ones, provide the touches which make Tom's escape plans possible; without these practical modifications the project would never have gotten as far as it did. Despite his ignorance and superstition, Jim displays an active intelligence, particularly in his relations with Huck and with other Negroes. It is only in the white man's world that he assumes completely the role of the docile, unthinking slave.

Tom Sawyer

In contrast to the individuality of Huck Finn and his rejection of the values of society, Tom Sawyer represents the values of the society from which Huck is escaping. On a superficial level, it would appear that Tom Sawyer is the more imaginative of the two, but Tom's oaths, his schemes, and his escapades are based upon books about romantic adventures which he has read. Whereas Huck has the ability and shrewdness to function outside of society, Tom Sawyer would founder. Huck is involved in real life, and Tom functions only when he is imitating something which he has read in a book. Tom's plans are always extravagant, absurd, or ridiculous while Huck's are simple, practical and shrewd.

Tom's conformity is seen in such events as when he makes Huck leave a nickle on the table for the candles, or when he makes Huck pay for the watermelon. These small facts lend credence to Huck's view that Tom Sawyer could not possibly help free a slave in the last section of the novel because of Tom's respectability and conformity to the views of his society.

Tom Sawyer's fantastic imagination lacks moral sense, and for this reason Tom often seems not quite real. He has generosity, it is true, but exercises it without personal involvement. His willingness to help Jim escape baffles even Huck. To Tom, all of life is a game—even what is grave. His refusal to take life seriously never changes. He has a profound influence over Huck, and he has a similar influence over Jim. The actions of Huck and Jim constantly need Tom's opinion as a guide or scale, whether he is present or not. Tom would never do anything in simple fashion if a more complicated scheme could be imagined. Tom appears to be too big for life until he is shot going over a fence. Only then does Tom Sawyer tend to be real.

Pap Finn

Huck's father is a totally despicable creature; drunken, brutal, and ignorant. He has no redeeming features except, perhaps, his ability to be independent. It is this ability to go it alone that has rubbed off on Huck.

Pap Finn resents his poverty, but his laziness will not let him do anything to overcome it. His festering resentment develops into a hatred of anyone who has anything—an education, a home, or a white shirt. An outstanding object of his hate (the memory of which evidently rankles most deeply) is a dignified Negro professor, his opposite in every way, whose very appearance is a reproach to Pap.

Huck comes in for a beating from Pap because he goes to school and will therefore become superior to his father. The widow and Judge Thatcher are safe from his violence, but he hates them bitterly because they prevent him from getting Huck's money. Unlike the other villains of the novel, the king and the duke, Pap has a sadistic streak and courts trouble. His violent death, therefore, is an appropriate touch of poetic justice.

Widow Douglas

One of the prosperous citizens of the town, the widow is kindly, understanding, and comparatively tolerant, but her standards of propriety always cause Huck to rebel. She never scolds Huck when she is displeased or disappointed, and when he misunderstands something she tries to explain it to him. When her sister Miss Watson plans to sell Jim, she tries to dissuade her from doing so. Huck genuinely likes the Widow Douglas and tries to please her, for he recognizes her sincerity.

Miss Watson

"A tolerable slim old maid with goggles on," Miss Watson is the opposite of her sister, Widow Douglas. She scolds, nags, and is easily out of patience. She believes in hellfire and damnation. Huck feels that in her Providence, "there wasn't no help for him anymore." Despite her pretensions to religion and the spiritual life, she plans to sell Jim for eight hundred dollars.

Judge Thatcher

Judge Thatcher had become the guardian of the boy's money at the end of *Tom Sawyer*. Prosperous and respected, he is also an astute man. When Huck dashes in and asks him to take back the six thousand dollars he owns, Judge Thatcher recognizes that something is afoot, and he ties up Huck's money legally so that it is safe. He feels morally and legally obligated to look after the money, and he frustrates Pap Finn's efforts to get his hands on it.

The Duke and the King

"The Duke of Bilgewater" and the "pore disappeared Dauphin, Looy the Seventeen" are simultaneously the funniest and the most detestable confidence men ever to grace the pages of a novel. Themselves quite ignorant and uneducated, they ply their questionable trade among country folk who are even more ignorant. These small-time charlatans are quite knowledgeable of the many human frailties. Thus they are able to sell worthless and even harmful patent medicines; they can turn to their advantage the religious gullibility of the country people; and they appeal to the lowest instincts of the villagers when they advertise *The Royal Nonesuch*. Yet, while the reader laughs at the victims, who often deserve what they get, he detests the two rogues for their utter heartlessness and amorality. It must be noted, however, that they are not violent men. They even use their cunning to keep Jim safe, although their reasons are obviously selfish ones.

The Grangerfords

The Grangerfords are typical of the pre-Civil War plantation aristocracy. They are religious and graciously hospitable, but they live by a perverted sense of family honor that makes them arrogant and gives them justification for killing those who have in some way violated their honor. Similar to the Grangerfords is the family they feud with, the Shepherdsons.

The Wilks Girls

The Wilks girls are among the very few admirable persons in the book. Redhaired Mary Jane is nineteen, and Huck responds to her frank, generous, and friendly nature. He admires her more than any girl he ever knew because, in his terms, she has "sand." Fourteen-year-old Joanna, the youngest, has a harelip. She is rather sharp and gives Huck a rough time when she questions him about the England he purports to come from. One senses in Huck a grudging admiration for her, for she is a relief among the gullibility that surrounds her. Susan, who is fifteen, endears herself to Huck because she chides Joanna for making a stranger uncomfortable. They are too trusting, and their ingenuous acceptance of the king and the duke almost ruins their lives.

The Phelpses

The Phelpses are about 45 or 50 and own "one of these little one-horse cotton plantations." They are gentle, unsuspecting souls; perfect victims for Tom's schemes. In addition to being a farmer, Uncle Silas is also a lay preacher. In their characters, Mark Twain underscores the fact that even such instinctively kind people were utterly indifferent to the immorality of slavery. Uncle Silas, for example, hopes to resell Jim and make a profit.

Aunt Polly

An important character in *Tom Sawyer*, Aunt Polly functions at the end only as a means of tying up loose ends. She will stand squarely for the conventional virtues, and she will make any sacrifice to maintain them. She is the voice of absolute order by society's standards.

GUIDE TO FREQUENCY OF APPEARANCE OF MAIN CHARACTERS BY GEOGRAPHIC LOCATION AND BOOK CHAPTER

Characters	St. Petersburg	Illinois A Hut on River	Jackson's Island	Down River Past St. Louis	Down River Near Cairo	Down River Kentucky	Down River Pokeville, Bricksville and South		Pikesville
	1-5	6-7	8-11	12-14	15-16	17-18	19-24	25-29	30-43
Huck Finn	✓	✓	✓	✓	✓	✓	✓	✓	✓
Jim	✓		✓	✓	✓		✓	✓	✓
Widow Douglas	✓								
Miss Watson	✓								
Tom Sawyer	✓								✓
Pap Finn	✓	✓							
Walter Scott Gang				✓					
Slave Hunters					✓				
Grangerfords						✓			
Shepherdsons						✓			
Colonel Sherburn							✓		
The Duke							✓	✓	
The King							✓	✓	
Mary Jane Wilks								✓	
The Phelps									✓
Aunt Polly									✓

58

CHARACTER DELINEATION CHART

	Huck Finn	Tom Sawyer	Jim	Pap Finn	Widow Douglas	Duke and King	Mary Jane Wilks
Role in novel	Protagonist.	Embodiment of white society, boyish life.	Touches the real, simple values.	Leads life of evil and waste. Stands for ignorance.	Stands for sincere idealism.	Provoke conflicts.	Innocent victim.
Character growth or change	Some; broadened understanding.	Little; perhaps at close.	None.	None.	None.	None.	None.
Principal actions	Narrator. Pilots raft down river. Saves Jim from capture, reveals frauds to Mary Jane, resolves personal morality.	Pulls Huck back to society at start and at close.	Befriends Huck, teaches him lore of nature and superstition, and meaning of friendship. Seeks his freedom.	Keeps Huck from education and society. Wants Huck's money.	Tries to give Huck true Christian values.	Devise swindles. King more ruthless.	Moves Huck to affection by her kindness.
Principal attributes	He has a strong moral sense, is a free spirit and a nonconformist. He is shrewd, loyal, kind and forgiving.	He is a prankster; playful, imaginative, unreal, unthinking, and generous.	He is whole; loving, patient, loyal, and simple.	He is ignorant; a drunkard who is vulgar and violent.	She is sincere, conventional, sympathetic, and religious.	They are corrupt, clever, daring, crude, ruthless, and amusing.	She is sensitive, pretty, and docile.

59

Questions and Answers on the Characters

Question 1.

Discuss character development in the novel.

Answer

None of the characters in the novel really changes very much. To suit the satirical purposes of the novel, many characters are mere types. Tom Sawyer certainly never changes and hardly develops. Even when hurt at the close of the novel, he goes on playing his same role. In almost weary fashion he pours out a total confession to his Aunt Polly in the form of triumph:

> "No, I ain't out of my HEAD; I know all what I'm talking about.
> We *did* set him free—me and Tom. We laid out to do it, and we
> *done* it. And we done it elegant, too." He'd got a start, and she
> never checked him up, just set and stared and stared, and let him
> clip along, and I see it warn't no use for *me* to put in.
>
> (Chapter 42)

Even Huck and Jim do not seem any different than they were at the start of the novel. One thing is for certain, though; we know them with great depth. We can say that all the characters in the novel tend to be flat. Only Huck and Jim tend to be round, but neither really surprises us.

Question 2.

What trait in Huck Finn does the novelist explore more than any other?

Answer

The novelist explores Huck's moral sense more than any other of his traits. In all of American literature no character ever considered moral decisions more than Huck Finn. He is hounded by moral reality:

> It was a close place. I took it up, and held it in my hand. I was
> a trembling, because I'd got to decide, forever, betwixt two things,
> and I knowed it. I studied a minute, sort of holding my breath,
> and then says to myself:
> "All right, then, I'll *go* to hell"—and tore it up.
>
> (Chapter 31)

Constantly he probes what is right and what is wrong; and more often than not, he doesn't know his own mind. Almost any choice for Huck is a severely moral choice and whatever he does can rarely be done without consternation:

> Mornings, before daylight, I slipped into corn fields and borrowed
> a watermelon, or a mushmelon, or a punkin, or some new corn,

or things of that kind. Pap always said it warn't no harm to borrow things, if you was meaning to pay them back, sometime; but the widow said it warn't anything but a soft name for stealing, and no decent body would do it.

(Chapter 12)

Question 3.
Describe an instance of epiphany in *Huckleberry Finn*.

Answer
If we take epiphany to mean a moment when a character learns something significant about himself, we can discuss an instance on the raft. Huck has returned from being lost in the fog. Jim is overjoyed at Huck's return. But Huck then pretends that he was never gone and that Jim was only dreaming. As if that deceit were not enough, Huck permits Jim to go on telling about the meaning of his dream in all its details. Huck then asks Jim what is the meaning of the trash. Jim looks straight at Huck and without smiling says,

> . . . En all you wuz thinkin 'bout wuz how you could make a fool uv ole Jim wid a lie. Dat truck dah is *trash*; en trash is what people is dat puts dirt on de head er day fren's en makes 'em ashamed.

(Chapter 15)

This incident and Jim's forthrightness forces Huck to humble himself. He knows now that to take advantage of the love of a friend in order to ridicule hurts more than anything else can.

Question 4.
How does the character of Huck Finn help the satire of the novel?

Answer
Huck's gentleness and general honesty with himself help to cushion many of the cruelties in the book. The amount of violence is appalling. But Huck's ability to accept people for what they are helps save the satire from being brutal invective. Huck's fascination with one event after another attracts the reader also, for Huck's attention to details and his own personality soften the effects of Southern brutality in the novel.

Question 5.
Do superstitions motivate the characters of *Huckleberry Finn*?

Answer
Superstitions move Huck and Jim all through the book. Before the first chapter is concluded, Huck sees a bad sign in a shrivelled-up spider which he flips off his shoulder. When he is with Jim, one superstitious belief after

another provides the material for most of their conversation and becomes a bond between them. Huck's seeing the special marks on the snow means that his father is back. As we become aware of the great number of references to superstition, we see that they affect Huck and the slaves in the book, but not the higher classes of society. Tom Sawyer finds his inspiration in reading. It would not be stretching the discussion too far to recognize that Tom Sawyer is bound in this world of romance as tightly as Jim and Huck are bound to primitive superstition. In this light, we can say that Tom Sawyer is superstitious in his addiction to the ways of outrageous romance. Neither his preference nor Huck's superstitions operate with true science or reason. However, both do make life exciting, and even poetic.

Plot

Huckleberry Finn is related to that class of novels called *picaresque*, which relate a series of adventures befalling a roguish hero who invariably manages to outwit all those who tangle with him.

Huckleberry Finn cannot be considered to be purely *picaresque*, however, because it is much more than a collection of adventures. Similarly, it cannot be viewed as a simple, linear story, such as that found in a typical detective novel, wherein the plot can be safely identified as a series of succeeding incidents and complications building to a climax of discovery.

Isolated incidents do not constitute a plot, and even a group of incidents thrown together do not necessarily make up a plot; it is only when incidents are selected and put together in a particular and meaningful manner that we begin to have plot. We may say then that *plot is developing purpose*.

In the simple detective novel we can easily pinpoint a particular arrangement of incidents, that is, the story-line, as being the plot, with the developing purpose being the movement towards the "discovery," which is often the unmasking of the villain. Twain's novel does not have such an easily identifiable plot. Where, then, can we find the developing purpose in *Huckleberry Finn*? We can argue that Jim's flight from slavery, along with the associated events leading to a resolution of Jim's fate, is a plot of sorts, but is it really the major plot? Or can we find the major plot in the series of incidents relating to Huck's moral dilemma of whether or not to return Jim to Miss Watson?

If we accept these two thin threads running through the novel as the main plot, then we are virtually forced to reject all the minor episodes, such as Huck's stay at the Grangerfords', as merely padding on the part of the author.

If we are to see the main plot of the book, we must consider the whole society that is portrayed, together with all the related elements of character, language, and the physical environment of the Mississippi River. It is really all these elements, alerting the emotions and judgment of the reader, in various combinations with one another, that make up the plot as a developing purpose. Another way of putting this would be to say that *Huckleberry Finn* is "poetic" rather than being a simple "action" novel.

Structure

It is not an oversimplification to say that the structure of a novel is the skeleton of the novel. A trip to a museum can show us the apparatus that determines what flesh can be hung on the rhinoceros or the ostrich. No skeleton will determine what the final being will resemble exactly; but flesh, feather, or hide cannot go far from the skeletal outline because it will be unsupported. In the same way a novel really is a highly involved complexity that is greater than the sum of its parts. We can speak of climax and anticlimax, or we can speak of parallels and contrasts in scenes; yet there is always more. To bend or misread any element of structure would distort the original. Therefore, our skeleton image does not fully explain structure. It does, however, give us a deep respect for the principles of things being held together.

The nature of structural elements may vary greatly from one novel to another. The main structural element in a novel can be, and often is, the plot. In one novel, the main structural element may be a story-line or sequence of events; in another novel, it may be simply an idea, a theme, or virtually any other literary device which holds the whole work together.

In *Huckleberry Finn*, the chronological sequence of events (note that the story does not jump back and forth in time) provides a measure of structure, but by and large, the novel acquires its structural unity from the point of view, the language, and the locale.

Because Huck is the narrator of the story we see everything through his eyes. Thus we judge circumstances and individuals as he does, most often, of course, to their disadvantage, since the instinctive sincerity in Huck contrasts strongly with the conscious and unconscious hypocrisy of those he meets during his journey. The point of view, therefore, is consistently maintained.

Similarly, the language of the novel is a unifying factor. As the narrator is the almost illiterate Huck, the language is highly ungrammatical, and the author spells a number of words phonetically so as to mirror the actual speech of the frontier. Often these spellings produce puns and ludicrous misuses of words that add a great deal of humor to the book.

A number of passages reflect Huck's sensitivity and awareness of the world around him. They have a folk lyricism, as in the description of the sky at night (Chapter 7), the thunderstorm (Chapter 8), and the dawn on the river (Chapter 19).

The third element that contributes to the unity of the novel (and some consider this to be the strongest factor of the three) is the locale—the benign, cruel, indifferent, sluggish, dangerous, grand Mississippi River that affects the lives of all the characters.

The river may be seen as a string supporting and holding together the episodes (the beads of our analogy) which take place on the river itself or on its banks. In a more general vein, the river also holds together a geo-graphical unit of local color, speech and customs, out of which, to a large extent, Twain has forged the many episodes of the novel.

Questions and Answers on Structure

Question 6.

What is the major difficulty in analyzing the structure of *Huckleberry Finn*?

Answer

The principal difficulty in analyzing *Huckleberry Finn* is the ending of the novel. Many critics seem to think that the plot sags at the end and that Tom Sawyer's appearance signifies loss of purpose. Even Ernest Hem-ingway, who gave this novel its greatest compliment, thought that the novel should have ended when Jim is taken from Huck. He thought that the rest of the book was cheating.

It does seem likely, nevertheless, that no other return to his society is possible for Huck unless a transition is made from the river to the families. Taking the factors of beginning, middle, and end, we can see that Mark Twain had a difficult problem before him. A book is not like life. Life goes on. A book must end. Conventional stories usually end when boy gets girl or when the bad guy gets shot. Twain's themes were quite complex, and his problem was to have the trip down the river end before Huck was spilled into the vast reaches of the Gulf. If Huck began a new life anywhere along the river, the book would have had many more chapters. If Huck suddenly was planted back in the presence of Aunt Polly or Miss Watson, unity would have been violated by abruptness. The reader would again be cheated. If it ended with the capture of Jim, as Hemingway suggested, it would have been tragic. Here, of course, we must digress for a moment. It is true that Huck is constantly in the presence of death. He begins his plans with a simulated murder. He sees a man about to be murdered on a wrecked steamboat. The carnage of death surrounds him in the feud. Boggs is shot dead in front of him. Also, Huck is lonesome. He begins the first chapter by telling us how lonesome he is. The miserable treatment of man by man repels him, even in the instance of two scoundrels getting what they deserve. Yet all of this does not add up to tragedy. The themes are not tragic because the vision of life that Huck enjoys is not tragic. To the reader, Huck's careful attempts to remain neutral may even be repugnant, as when he permits the duke and the king to sell a family down the river. But in no other way can Huck go on in this life. His refusal to be responsible, to identify with others, often causes more harm than involvement would. But this is precisely what gives Huck his optimism. Only gradually can Huck end where he started in this novel. The shenanigans of Tom Sawyer, offensive as they are to our belief in Jim's sense of loyalty, make sense only if we realize that that is the world to which Huck must return. Mark Twain knows no other for him and Huck knows no other. On the last page of the novel, Huck knows that the world of Aunt Sally and Aunt Polly is still not for him. He will head out for the Territory.

In conclusion, we can say that no effort can make the difficulties disappear. The ending does not really *satisfy* anyone. The best we can do is accept it. We can deplore the *deus ex machina* that sets Jim free. It seems astounding that Miss Watson should conveniently die. She appeared to be hale and hearty. It is incredible that she should set Jim free. We have not the slightest idea of her motivation. The structure sags, but only because it did take something like a miracle to set any black man free in the 1840's.

Question 7.

Can the novel be said to have a symbolic structure?

Answer

Certain authors, notably Milton, Whitman, and Mark Twain, very markedly give impressions of themselves in their work, despite the reader's efforts to see the work by itself. *Huckleberry Finn* reveals much of the nature of Samuel Clemens, and for this reason the question can be answered in two ways.

The structure of *Huckleberry Finn* has the strong suggestion of Clemens' private thoughts and aversions throughout. At the front of the book Mark Twain has written, ''. . . persons attempting to find a plot in it will be shot.'' If the book is taken solely as a socio-historical narrative, it succeeds brilliantly and presents no difficulties. By taking the novel in this way, we would have to say that Clemens simply reminisced and offered a series of loosely connected yarns to give a picture of life along the Mississippi in the 1840's. Mark Twain suggests this himself when he warns us to look for no plot. Such an interpretation would solve many problems of structure. Why, for example, do we have the Sherburn incident? Of what effect on the purposes of Huck or Jim is the wreck of the *Walter Scott* or the Grangerford-Shepherdson feud? Taking the answer that each incident serves to give a more complete view of the river life, we must look, then, into the vision of the world held by Clemens and thereby see the threads of unity weaving his view of this world, as offered by the inhabitants along the Mississippi in 1845. To that end we can examine the satire of the book, and we immediately perceive that any incident which fails to belong closely to any plot structure usually deals with the theme of man's inhumanity to man. The book actually takes on a symbolic structure based on the moral vision and interests of the author. His protagonist will not be free. He will be free to follow only the purpose of the author. The victimized puppet will never know where he is going next. Wherever it will be, he knows he will see more cruelty. He will not be able to change his world. Mark Twain presented such characters in his later novels, such as *The Mysterious Stranger*. The complexities of such a study of the structure of *Huckleberry Finn* are enormous, yet sufficiently consistent to present a scheme of the world view held by Clemens. In this way we can account for every episode in the book as it relates to the personality of Clemens and his other works. Such a study is mostly biographical, yet it would produce a grand symbolic structure. Since such a study would also be psychological, we should look at another possible symbolic structure.

To maintain the points we have made above in the first part of this discussion, we should try to retain the unity of the novel and eliminate the problem of permitting the author's personality to determine the course of our discussion. Immediately we can see that the river remains. More than one critic has seen the symbolic nature of the river holding the novel together. The river can be taken in a mythic sense. Any myth transmits by story that which lurks behind conceptual knowledge. The very things that we know best are the things that we will not or cannot utter. It appears that mind and soul are one when man reaches this mythic center. All about the river, in the mumbojumbo of Jim's rituals for snakebite and the superstitions of Huck himself, we see the mystery of another existence different from the Christian norms of society. The river can be taken as a god with all the absolute largess and wrath belonging to a god. Men along the river become small. Away from the river there is no other life. The river stretches endlessly north and endlessly south. Such a structural conception lends itself to an infinite number of interpretations and relationships which deal with initiation, guilt, redemption, and reward.

To pursue this point briefly, as it relates to Huck: Huck can be taken as making a journey of initiation. The principle of this initiation is not important. It can be initiation into manhood, it can be initiation into society. There will be renewal, restoration, rejuvenation. The initiation can also come in a journey to God. God can be paradise, or peace, or freedom. The journey can also be an earnest or burning desire to make sense out of this world we are born into. It can also be a need to unite the imperfections of the real world with the perfect harmony of the imagined or spiritual world. Twain has said in *Life on the Mississippi* that he simply wanted to expose Huck to different facets of life on the river. These experiences suggest the same nonsense of any initiation—no immediate purpose, merely trial. Trial of passage is trial to move to a higher state or a higher reality. Huck's own faked murder at the outset begins the movement. The details in between, until his being reborn at the Wilkses as Tom Sawyer, are fairly obvious. The peace of the river, the shore that represents slavery, are fairly consistent. The river does become a god in this symbolic sense of refuge, peace, paradise, and freedom.

Question 8.

What is the significance of certain repetitions that occur in the novel?

Answer

These repetitions can be related to structure and have been by various critics. Such repetitions, when analyzed, add a beguiling unity to the novel. Whether or not Mark Twain was consciously aware of these repetitions cannot be ascertained. If the moral choices of the participants are wrong choices deliberately made, we can see that only disaster can follow. That is to say, the same event can have a different motivation. The reason for doing the thing matters most. The choices of the duke and the king certainly lead them to extract total gain where gold alone is not enough. The same is true of the lost men on the *Walter Scott*. They return for some trifling amount on the person of their victim. Their return makes possible Huck and Jim's escape from the wreck but seals their own fate on the wreck like that of their victim. The greed of the gang permits Huck and Jim to be safe. Even the obvious repetition of the duke and the king in repeating the Royal Nonesuch teaches them a horrible lesson. Most repetitions are not so obvious but do establish a rhythm in the structure. The gullibility of crowds, the desertion of comrades in danger, the relevancy of snakes, the significance of drunkenness, find correspondences and meaning in various parts of the novel. Objects and even words and phrases have particular unifying effects in various places or contexts of the novel. The poignant story that Jim tells of his deaf child not hearing a door slam after her supposed disobedience is soon juxtaposed with the duke playing the role of a deaf-mute. What is real in the service of self-knowledge can be a sham in the services of abuse. The pulse of moral purpose is contrasted in the repetition.

Meaning

No poem, play, or novel can have a final or inescapable meaning, simply because each work of art requires an audience. The introduction of audience or reader immediately produces different effects if only because no two people respond in exactly the same way. Each reader is a creator. His response participates in the creative act of the author. But he can never be the author in mind and heart; therefore large or small differences of opinion will exist in all readers. However, to say that there are differences is not to say that there is no meaning. All that can be asked of us is that we be able to articulate our own response to a novel or poem. Most obviously, a close reading of the work would suggest the most number of meanings and the most acceptable meanings.

Our own sense of decorum will also color our response to a novel. There are people who directly identify with characters in a novel. There are others who are repelled by the style of the author's writing. Beyond such considerations there remains the matter of learning from literature. It is true that reading is not a substitute for living. However, if a person is alone in his own world going through the repetitive process of daily activity, reading will exercise his faculties to learn about other people and other things. Analyzing a novel can make us analyze our own lives. The conduct of our own lives will help determine our response to a novel. Our own needs will help us to see one theme or another in the work.

The most likely beginning of an analysis of meaning can be with theme. Is there one central idea in this novel? Are there several ideas that suggest themselves? Would anyone think that my idea of the theme is believable? Am I pressing too hard and reading things into the novel? Such questions can assist the student in his analysis of theme. A more basic question, even, might simply be: what was the author trying to do? We must remember, however, that any statement of theme must be supported by specific evidence from the novel. We should look for themes which would have a general acceptance and leave strange interpretations to those who do not care about adequately supporting their contentions.

Of the many themes which run throughout the novel, several are introduced in the first chapter. First, Huck mentions that the Widow Douglas wanted to "sivilize" him. In contrast, Huck wants to escape and be "free and satisfied." The conflict between society and the individual becomes a controlling theme as the novel develops, and is investigated on several different levels. Furthermore, the novel ends with Huck planning "to light out" for a different territory because Aunt Sally plans to "sivilize" him. In between these opening and closing remarks, Huck encounters varying aspects, attitudes, and restrictions of society and learns to prefer his own individual freedom. This idea will receive its dramatic climax when Huck decides to oppose the dictates of society and "go to hell" for the sake of his friendship with Jim.

The restriction of living with the Widow Douglas also introduces the idea of Huck's quest for freedom, which will later be correlated with Jim's quest of freedom from slavery. This theme also functions on many levels as Huck and Jim make their way down the river in search of freedom.

In conjunction with the restrictive effects of civilization is Twain's subtle satire on the traditional concepts of religion. Huck sees Miss Watson's traditional view of "a pearly gate" concept of heaven as being essentially boring and restrictive. The Widow Douglas' view is somewhat more appealing, but Huck would prefer to go to a more exciting place. The concept of religion, in general, throughout the novel is attacked by Twain in various guises. Basically, a society which required its property (its slaves) to become practising Christians is a contradiction of the tenets of Christianity. Slaves were sometimes referred to, ironically, as "baptized property." For Twain, the concept of slavery and the pious religious concepts of the southerners were the height of contradictory absurdity.

Another theme introduced in the first chapter is that of Huck's birth and rebirth. When he feels stifled or deadened by society, he escapes to become reborn again. And throughout the novel Huck loses his identity, assumes different names (even Tom Sawyer's), arranges his own murder, and then, in turn, is reborn with new or different values.

Furthermore, each time that Huck escapes from some situation, the theme of his loneliness and isolation is often touched upon. In the first chapter, he says that "I felt so lonesome I most wished I was dead." Man's feeling of loneliness and isolation is a recurrent theme in all of Twain's works. In this novel, it is expressed by Huck's encounter with the vastness of the frontier, with the magnitude of the Mississippi River and with the formidable forests which surrounded the settlements. This feeling of loneliness is also correlated with the superstitions which permeate the novel. Confronted with the vastness of their isolation, Huck, Jim, and other characters put great reliance on superstitions of one sort or another. These superstitions develop into an important motif as the novel develops.

A reader has difficulty finding any character, with some very minor exceptions, free from some vice or corruption. Almost every aspect of human ugliness is satirized: greed, cruelty, gullibility, lynching, hysterical religion, lechery, prudery, antiquated codes of behavior, war, stupidity, and many more. Miss Watson, for example, believes herself to be above worldly temptation, but the eight hundred dollars offered for Jim breaks her down. The boatman is reluctant to do anything about the people who are supposedly marooned on the *Walter Scott* until he realizes he may get a reward. The Grangerfords and Shepherdsons, because they follow a senseless and antiquated code, become veritable butchers. The only essentially disinterested and humane individuals are Huck and Jim. The basic difference between them and the other characters is that they bear no allegiance to organized society and its demands; Jim because he is a slave, and Huck because he is a "river rat." All the other characters are subject to the laws and codes, judicial and moral, of their society, and their beliefs and actions are controlled, not by their naturally decent instincts, but by these artificial codes. Mark Twain's overall theme, therefore, seems to be that organized society somehow corrupts man's naturally decent instincts and perverts his behavior. One can already see, in the themes of this book the inroads of that pessimism that was later to dominate all of its author's beliefs.

Questions and Answers on Meaning

Question 9.
What is the principal theme of *The Adventures of Huckleberry Finn*?

Answer
Huckleberry Finn proposes a theme so fundamental as to be disarmingly simple. The entire novel constantly supports the efforts of Huck and Jim to live their own lives free of the restraints of compulsion. Jim's situation needs little elaboration. He is a slave in a society that knows no freedom for him unless he can escape to the free states or buy his freedom. Since Jim is undoubtedly the worst manager of money that ever appeared in fiction, being totally unaccustomed to having any, he can only flee. It is noteworthy that Jim had no thought of freedom until he was about to be sold down the river. His flight starts out in reasonable fashion but after passing Cairo, flight becomes only a vague memory. Almost the same fate awaits Huck. Huck cannot abide "sivilization," as he would call it. The conventional ways of society, particularly in matters of religious practices, to Huck are nothing but going through the motions. Not only is his soul unaffected by religious thought, his very reason is affronted by the contradictons or insufficiencies which he sees in religion. He can adjust to the ways of school life, and he can wear uncomfortable clothes. But his instincts are out of tune with what is expected of him. His free spirit can resort to escape only because he knows that he cannot fight an opponent that cannot be overcome. Huck longs to be free of his whole past—Pap, the Widow, St. Petersburg, school attendance, Bible lessons, and all attachments. His flight, of course, has no immediate objective. He starts out with the notion of going fifty miles down the river, but travels eleven hundred miles down the river, and ends exactly where he started, back in the world of Tom Sawyer. Jim and Huck lose their search, except that Jim is saved by an act of God in Miss Watson's death. Huck can only hope to fly again to the open and free territory.

Question 10.
What is the relation of satire to meaning in the novel?

Answer
A great portion of *Huckleberry Finn* is concerned solely with satire. Some of Mark Twain's targets are concrete, others are grand and abstract. Twain's attacks on the people in the small towns along the river brutally

satirize the lives which they live. Two outstanding examples are the conduct of people in the Sherburn incident, and the families in the feud. In the Sherburn affair, Mark Twain ruthlessly singles out the cowardice of a mob before one man with a shotgun. With almost fiendish delight Sherburn abuses the leader of the mob and every man, or half-man, in it. Where a few sentences would have served, the sureness of the satirist's hand continues the beating even after the mob has capitulated. The feud of the Shepherdsons and the Grangerfords satirizes itself in utter futility with the death of mere children. Here, the satirist found much to redeem the Grangerfords, especially in their self-discipline and fine taste; but affection gives way to the truth of their latent blindness of purpose.

The larger satirical themes deal mostly with the whole romantic concept and the abuse of religious belief. These abstract ideas of religious belief and the romantic ideal are assaulted over and over in *Huckleberry Finn*. The most polished attack on the romantic ideal is in the recollection of Emmeline Grangerford with her gruesome poems, her paintings, and her room. Throughout the book, outward religious practices and creeds are presented as baffling or contradictory. Ministers are hopeless, and "pre-foreordestination" and can never be unravelled.

It is worthy to note that after Huck and Jim pass Cairo and lose any hope of a plan for freedom, satire becomes a major thematic element. The coat-of-arms and Tom Sawyer's four mournful inscriptions demonstrate Mark Twain's ability to carry his war against the romantic ideal to the point of childishness.

Question 11.
Relate violence and suffering in the novel.

Answer
In view of the great number of instances in which people are hurt badly, there seems to be little suffering in the novel. The feud between the Shepherdsons and the Grangerfords would be one example. Despite the loss of sons before Huck's arrival, and despite the death of fine, handsome men at the steamboat loading dock, none of the women in the novel seem touched by the violence. Even Huck does not linger over the loss of Buck Grangerford. We can only account for the lack of suffering by focusing on Huck's youth. Young people are not touched for long by events. However, Huck is touched when others are not. He grieves over the treatment of the duke and the king when no one else will. He even tries to aid the murderers on the *Walter Scott*. But despite these instances of concern, most of the people in the novel never suffer. The closest we come to suffering in any convincing form is in Mary Jane's crying over the lost slave family, separated by the sale, and Aunt Sally's sitting up all night waiting for Tom Sawyer to be found. In both instances Huck dramatically alters his plans. In the first

instance he tells Mary Jane of the fraudulent pair; in the second instance he obeys in not searching for Tom and Jim, his only friends. The voyage down the river has made it impossible for Huck to see where people are really hurting, or else Mark Twain was not interested in doing more than pointing out the foibles of man and his capacity for violence. For in spite of the violence, no one in the novel is hurt in any meaningful or abiding way. Young Miss Boggs sees her father murdered before her eyes, but she gets no attention, by way of grief, from Huck. Huck watches Boggs die, and then moves on to the circus, stopping only to watch Colonel Sherburn confront the mob. Perhaps the river dwarfed man, or Twain's vision of man.

Style

In discussing style it would be possible to have an almost infinite number of categories or components whereby we could account for the particular manner of an author. How the author arranges his words might be the first thought regarding style, but style involves the actual texture of words and phrases and clauses in the book. The "best" style is that which matches the words to ideas. It is actually the soul of the author revealing his peculiar gifts in his work. A dancer, a baseball player, an actor, or a singer may have a style that sets him apart from all others. Yet how difficult it is to say what makes one particular artist so very different. We can begin to analyze style only by dividing it into such elements as diction, imagery and symbolism, syntax, emphasis, point of view, subjectivity and tone.

Any discussion of style usually begins with diction because diction involves only the writer's choice of words. If we paraphrase the work of some author, especially a fine poet, it is not hard to see how more apt or more beautiful the poet's original work remains. Our own may say what the poet says, but not so well. The aptness of his words was Mark Twain's great achievement. He knew the right word could produce the effect of humor or of seriousness or both. He knew a word could be inflated or ordinary; it could be appealing or repugnant. Much of the emotional impact of Twain's work comes through his use of words.

Another element which determines style is the use of imagery and symbolism. Imagery concerns itself with the discussion of representations of things in a more narrow sense than with symbolism. Imagery gives a picture which best suggests a meaning, but symbolism is concerned with larger meanings. Images employ figurative language for poetic or rhetorical effect. When an image suggests more than it states, it becomes a symbol. Symbols evolve more slowly, as do their effects. Symbols often represent the unknown world of what cannot be articulated, and perhaps what cannot be conceptualized. In this sense, the Mississippi River may be seen as a major symbol in the book.

Yet another facet of style is syntax. Sentence structure suggests the mechanical arrangement of elements in a sentence. We can call the elements words, phrases, and clauses. We can also add that there are types of sentences. Anyone slightly familiar with the sentences of Ernest Hemingway and those of Henry James can see, first of all, considerable differences in the length of the sentences. Even the rhythm of their style will be determined by syntax. Variety of effect can be achieved by sentence structure.

No element of style can be more important to the humorist than emphasis. By emphasis he knows when to say something, how long to dwell upon it, and whether or not to repeat it. Another way of expressing emphasis would be to call it timing. Emphasis is related to the method of development, to the amount of space given to an idea, and to the number of details an author will include.

Point of view can also add to the style of a novel. In order to tell a story we need a storyteller. The author himself can be the narrator. He may prefer to keep himself out of any part of the story. In this instance we usually say he takes the point of view of omniscience. He knows what is in the minds of all the characters. If the story is told by someone who is involved in the action, we find a different effect. When one of the characters tells the story we usually find a closer proximity to the places and actions of the story. A neutral narrator such as Huck can serve to give a relatively objective account of incidents in a novel, but the personal attitudes of the author can never be completely eliminated from any work. A pure objectivity is impossible just because of selection made by the author. But few authors try to be totally objective. Those who do may appear to achieve it in their style; however, the total effect often turns out to be monstrously subjective. Mark Twain, being a humorist, had to include his philosophy in his work. What is he for? What is he against? These attitudes will help to shape his novel.

Tone is another important element of style. Tone suggests mood. Since writing is an art and art involves the emotional and aesthetic effect, tone used artistically can match emotion with subject matter. Put most simply, tone can be said to represent the attitude the author wants the reader to take toward his subject. In Chapter 19, for example, Twain gives a description of the Mississippi River at dawn in a very idyllic tone:

Not a sound, anywheres—perfectly still—just like the whole world was asleep, only sometimes the bull-frogs a-cluttering, maybe.

Mark Twain revolutionized the use of language in fiction. Critics have noted that perhaps his greatest service to American literature was using his genius to put natural speech into a literary form. It had been assumed that common speech, particularly that of uneducated individuals, was far too inexpressive for projecting subtleties of emotion. Mark Twain proved, and *Huckleberry Finn* is an extraordinary example of this, that the vulgar tongue could, in the hands of a master, express anything the writer demanded of it. The book is written chiefly in Huck's Pike County dialect. However, the language undergoes subtle shifts as each character enters the picture. Mark Twain's explanatory note about the dialects, which is at the beginning of every edition of the novel, is to be taken seriously:

In this book a number of dialects are used, to wit: the Missouri negro dialect; the extremest form of the backwoods South-Western dialect; the ordinary "Pike-County" dialect; and four modified varieties of this last. The shadings have not been done in a haphazard fashion, or by guess-work; but painstakingly, and with the trustworthy guidance and support of personal familiarity with these several forms of speech.

STYLE CHART

THEMES	DICTION	IMAGERY	TONE
Freedom for Jim	Jim's language can frighten Huck; e.g., "buy" or "steal" his wife, or "get Ab'litionist" to help.		Always a vague reality, always further from his grasp until hopeless and absurd.
Freedom for Huck	Huck's expressions of disgust with the "sivilizing" process are ludicrous.	Huck's idea of freedom is having necessities of life, peace, and harmony.	Searching, skeptical, evasive, pragmatic.
Friendship of Huck and Jim	Rite of passage terms, Chap. 15 Jim—"got down on my knees en kiss yo' foot; " Huck—"I could almost kissed his foot." Much superstitious idiom.	Huck learns the design of the cosmos from Jim— "An astronomical theory." Jim uses poetry to answer ultimate questions.	
Friendship of Huck and Tom	Huck admires Tom but cannot understand his silliness. He constantly uses self-deprecating expressions when with Tom. Tom usually fanciful.		Fanciful, imaginative, incredible, foolish.
Mystique of river	Huck, of course, provides the lyrical passages of sound and sight along river.	Most poetic passages of river expressed in awe of its majesty and power.	Idyllic.
Satire		River communities satirized in brutal, direct images of disgust towards mobs, willing dupes, and lazy inhabitants.	Complete range from wistful to violent.

EMPHASIS	HUCK AS NARRATOR POINT OF VIEW	MARK TWAIN SUBJECTIVITY
Reaches high point when even Huck is afraid of implications for Huck.	Lives with ambivalence in moral choices. Accepts each morality temporarily, but fails to understand Tom's helping Jim to escape.	To the extent that Twain is involved as much as Huck in moral ambivalence, he cannot solve problem of Jim's freedom except by death of Mrs. Watson.
Huck's need to be unfettered opens and closes the book. He could live with anyone. All accept him.	Movement his sole delight. He avoids attachments, yet suffers loneliness.	Twain realizes that Huck cannot be alone with his loneliness, and he cannot live with the evils of society. This dilemma never fully resolved in the novel.
When Jim speaks out against abuse for his believing Huck, Huck apologizes.	Respects Jim and always speaks of his common sense despite his status. Amused by Jim's stubbornness.	The author gives complete freedom to Jim to be himself with Huck, his only friend in the world.
The complete trust—almost too ridiculous—that Huck gives Tom in the rescue of Jim.	Always confused by Tom's proposals. Knows what to expect from Tom, but feels subordinate to him.	Tom Sawyer's striding through the last part of the novel is a near disaster. Mark Twain saw him as necessary to represent conventions.
Often Huck stresses that life on a raft is beautiful. He constantly realizes the need for peace on the raft.	Lives the reality of the river, but does not see beyond the moment. No past.	The years as a river boat pilot gave Mark Twain a great love of river life whose idyllic details are often found in Huck's reveries.
Strongest emphasis is overt in gullibility of characters, and subtle when feud follows sermon on brotherly love, or wreck of *W. Scott*.	Huck has a wit and understanding beyond his years but not beyond our acceptance. He often fails to see significance of his observations.	Twain's personal knowledge of the world gave novel much violence, but enough optimism in Huck's tone.

Questions and Answers on Style

Question 12.

What is the importance of the point of view in *The Adventures of Huckleberry Finn*?

Answer

The story of *Huckleberry Finn* is told from the point of view of Huck Finn himself. Huck goes from one adventure to another with the eyes of an inexperienced boy. Naturally, his responses are not those of a grown man, and therefore an innocence pervades the entire novel. The charm of Huck's innocence gives most force to the novel's sure movement. If Huck had seen the full significance of each experience, the book would have bogged down in the cruelty and violence that fill it. But things bounce off Huck to the point that he can go from the death of Boggs, to the scene at Sherburn's yard, and then to the circus. He doesn't brood over each situation. This method permits the book to cover a range of incidents in swift fashion. The fact that the story is told from the point of view of Huck Finn was because Clemens had waited for a suitable character to come to his mind who could carry a novel through to its conclusion in the first person. He knew when he was writing *Tom Sawyer* that Tom could never do it, but Huck probably could. His choice of Huck altered the path of American fiction.

Question 13.

Briefly discuss tone in *Huckleberry Finn*.

Answer

It would not be an exaggeration to say that all of this novel could be analyzed by tone and those things related to tone. It is a triumph of tonal unity through point of view, variety, diction, satire, and incident. Briefly, we can say that the freshness of the novel is its glory. This consistent newness comes about because of Huck himself. He is alive, he is curious, he is aware. As he moves from one adventure to another, he personally becomes involved and, boylike, tells the reader how he is seeing these things for the first time. But more importantly, Huck's personal style can establish tone with just a few words. We need no examples here because the book can be opened to any page to find Huck's narrative line establishing tone, or shifts of tone, with lightning speed. Some of the greatest achievements of tonal unity and shifts of tone occur when Huck attends the circus, when he prepares his own murder, when he looks out at the stars with Jim, or when he says his lone farewell to Mary Jane. Any one of these instances shows the consistency of the mood for each, while each instance is distinct in tone from any other. Mark Twain threw himself completely into Huck's position and told of the world as Huck saw it—ever new.

Question 14.
Discuss the use of humor in *Huckleberry Finn*.

Answer
Most of the humor of the novel comes straight out of the tradition of humor in the West. Time and again we see Huck as the Mississippi River's greatest yarn spinner. Huck can make up stories for every situation. His willingness to lie cannot be judged harshly because comedy invariably insulates against grave morality. When we laugh at something, we reserve our moral judgment. In one ridiculous situation after another we hear Huck tell some fantastic story as he does with the two slave hunters, who are so convinced that Huck's "family" have smallpox that they give him forty dollars to move down the river. The burlesque of the French language provides amusing moments as Huck tries to justify even the existence of such a language. Huck's ridicule of the romantic ideal of Emmeline Grangerford hits its mark. Hyperbole, or exaggeration, of such outrageous proportions amuses us as Huck describes dogs, or rats, or people. The tobacco-chewing men of the dirty Arkansas town merit scorn. The buffoonery of the king and the duke is unmatched in American fiction. Huck's knowledge of history confuses everyone but Huck. Burlesque begins and ends the novel. Low comedy abounds: puns, misquotations, incongruities, and gross comparisons.

Question 15.
Discuss the diction of *Huckleberry Finn*.

Answer
Time and again critics marvel over the sustained creation of Huck's vernacular style which is used to narrate the story. In his amusing explanation at the front of his book, Mark Twain tells us that a number of dialects will appear. He says, "I make this explanation for the reason that without it many readers would suppose that all these characters were trying to talk alike and not succeeding." No one before had attempted a long narrative with such success. Huck talks as he always talked. He rarely fails to tell what is happening. The only long interruption comes when Colonel Sherburn addresses the crowd. When Huck speaks, he is startlingly concrete. His images of sound and sight are not unnecessarily embellished:

Every night we passed towns, some of them away up on black hillsides, nothing but just a shiny bed of lights, not a house could you see. The fifth night we passed St. Louis, and it was like the whole world lit up. In St. Petersburg they used to say there was twenty or thirty thousand people in St. Louis, but I never believed it till I see that wonderful spread of lights at two o'clock that still night. There warn't a sound there; everybody was asleep.

His freedom of expression ignores any rules of correctness, as when he watches the ferryboat "smell around the wreck for Miss Hooker's remainders." Mark Twain used the system of saying his words over and over to himself before writing. Here, his skill as a storyteller served him well. He made the careful distinctions between *ain't* and *hain't* by combining a tuned ear with the humorist's ability to mimic speech. So consistent is Twain's judgment that we can choose any example to match speech and action. The king, as a fraud, talking about "funeral orgies" matches perfectly in burlesque the "English" poser outrageously sure of himself and the people's willing gullibility. More than truth comes out of the page. Its best effect comes by reading it aloud.

*Themes in *Huckleberry Finn*

It is no secret that Mark Twain had difficulty in writing *Huckleberry Finn*. He wrote about half of it and then put the manuscript away to gather dust for almost seven years; yet the finished whole seems easy, simple, natural. Huck, the unifying thread that ties everything together, gains in stature by having no taller rivals near him—only the river tramps who impose themselves on his generosity and the hunted Negro whom he befriends.

In spite of its episodic nature, the book falls naturally into three thematic units. In the first sixteen chapters the theme has to do with what is of and from St. Petersburg: Huck, Tom, Nigger Jim, and Pap. The second thematic unit includes the most strongly satiric, the most powerful part of the book, bringing Huck and Jim into contact with the outside world. In the cross-section of the South through which they journey, Huck witnesses the Grangerford-Shepherdson feud, the chicanery of the king and the duke, the killing of Boggs, Colonel Sherburn's quelling of the mob, and finally the village funeral. The characters of the king and the duke add to the thematic unity of this section. The third thematic unit is short, a sort of coda to the rest, covering the period at the Phelps farm in which Tom re-enters the story. This section repeats the romanticized motif of the first part and thus brings the book around full-circle, before its close.

The art of characterization is the one most important to a novelist, and Mark Twain's characters are his greatest literary achievement. Something of his method in characterization may be learned from a passage he wrote in 1907:

> Every man is in his own person the whole human race, with not a detail lacking. I am the whole human race without a detail lacking; I have studied the human race with diligence and strong interest all these years in my own person; in myself I find in big or little proportions every quality and every defect that is findable in the mass of the race.

This suggests that when he had need of a certain trait, his habit was to dig for it within himself, to isolate and study it, then to enlarge it to the proporation proper to the character in question. This suggestion is borne out by a marginal note in one of his books: "If Byron—if any man—draws 50 characters, they are all himself—50 shades, 50 moods, of his own character. And when the man draws them well, why do they stir my admiration? Because they are me—I recognize myself."

A careful study of *Huckleberry Finn* shows that it is the characters and their interrelationship which determine the arrangement and structure of the

*Editor's title. By Gladys Carmen Bellamy. From "Acceptance versus Rejection" in *Mark Twain as a Literary Artist*, University of Oklahoma Press, 1950.

book. The three thematic sections subdivide into little units notable for the contrast they offer each other. The first three chapters continue, naturally enough, the vein of *Tom Sawyer*, to which this book becomes a sort of sequel. Everything is colored by the excitement of Tom's imaginary adventures; he insists on doing all things according to the books he has read, from having his Gang sign in blood their oaths of allegiance to capturing and holding people for ransom. Ben Rogers, A Gang member, wants to know what being "ransomed" means, and Tom replies:

> "I don't know. But that's what they do. I've seen it in books; and of course that's what we've got to do."
> "But how can we do it if we don't know what it is?"
> "Why, blame it all, we've *got* to do it. Don't I tell you it's in the books? Do you want to go to doing different from what's in the books and get things all muddled up?"

And here, in a simple argument among boys, Mark Twain sets the pattern for this, his greatest story, as a satire on institutionalism. The three figures, Tom, Huck and Jim, represent three gradations of thought and three levels of civilization. Tom, pretending so intensely that it becomes so, says we can't do it except as in the books. Is this what civilization really is— merely a pretense according to a set pattern? Tom is on the highest level, in the sense of being most civilized; but he represents a mawkish, romantic, artificial civilization. Compared with him, Nigger Jim and Huck are primitives; and the closer Mark Twain gets to primitivism, the better his writing becomes. He shows us the African in Jim, imbuing him with a dark knowledge that lies in the blood and his nerve ends. Huck Finn stands between these two; he is the "natural man," suggesting Walt Whitman's dream of the great American who should be simple and free. Both Tom and Jim are in bondage to institutionalism.[1] Tom can't do anything against the rules of his books; Jim can't do anything against the rules of his taboos, his voodoo fears and charms and superstitions. Only Huck is free of institutions. Tom and Jim are always sure they are right, since each has his institution to consult and to follow; but Huck is tormented by doubts. When he is with Tom, he is willing to join Tom in following the books; when he is with Jim, he is careful not to break Jim's taboos, especially after the incident of the rattlesnake skin. But when Huck is alone, because he has no rules to go by he is guided by the voice within himself. He listens to what goes on inside him. He is free to probe within his own heart, where is to be found whatever bit of divinity man has—what we know as his soul.

If *Tom Sawyer* is accepted as a satire against the moralizing Sunday school tales, *Huckleberry Finn* has a much broader field as a satire against institutionalism in general. The institution of slavery is basic in this book, just as it is in *Pudd'nhead Wilson*. In *A Connecticut Yankee*, Mark Twain fulminates against church and state. In *Joan of Arc* he attacks the oppressions of formal religion and formal law. In *Hadleyburg* he frowns upon the institutionalism by which young people are trained in hypocrisy and the forms of empty "honor." Indeed, he sees the village itself as an institution—the tight little institution of the mores of the folk, which dictates the condemnation of all outlanders and innovators.

Within each of the thematic units in *Huckleberry Finn* there is a subtle variation of character and atmosphere. After the idyllic, romantic atmosphere which permeates the first three chapters, in the next four the story veers sharply from the mood of *Tom Sawyer*, and Pap takes the stage, drunken and disreputable, feeling himself the victim of sundry social ills. Into this satiric portrait went Mark Twain's years of observation of mountain whites, piney-woods people, and river rats. Pap is completely revealed through his oration on the "guv'ment." This unit ends when Huck flees because he fears his father will kill him in a fit of delirium tremens.

After so much violence, Jackson's Island gives him a feeling of peace. He explores the island, and just as he begins to feel lonely he discovers Jim, a Negro who has run away from home because his owner is planning to sell him "down to Orleans"—the Negro's equivalent of hell. Thereafter the runaway slave and the outcast waif share the island and comfort each other. This small unit of four chapters, the interlude on Jackson's Island, ends once more in the threat of violence and fear. Men are approaching the island to search for Jim.

Mark Twain's prefatory note warns the reader that seven different dialects are used in the book; the shadings among them are so fine that not every reader can perceive them, and he does not want readers to think that "all these characters were trying to talk alike and not succeeding." His sensitivity to speech enabled him to say, "The shadings have not been done in haphazard fashion, or by guesswork, but painstakingly." But the artistry of such shadings in dialect fades before his skill in employing the vernacular of Huck Finn for a book-length narrative. Huck has a strong, vivid, natural imagination—not an artificial one, such as Tom's, or a superstitious one, such as Jim's. He describes, with memorable effect, a summer storm which he and Jim watched from the security of their cave on the island:

> . . . it looked all blue-black outside, and lovely; and the rain would thrash along by so thick that the trees off a little ways looked dim and spider-webby; and here would come a blast of wind that would bend the trees down and turn up the pale underside of the leaves; and then a perfect ripper of a gust would follow along and set the branches to tossing their arms as if they was just wild; and next, when it was just about the bluest and blackest—*fst!* it was as bright as glory, and you'd have a little glimpse of tree-tops a-plunging about away off yonder in the storm, hundreds of yards further than you could see before; dark as sin again in a second, and now you'd hear the thunder let go with an awful

crash, and then go rumbling, grumbling, tumbling, down the sky towards the under side of the world, like rolling empty barrels down stairs—where it's long stairs and they bounce a good deal, you know.

Mark Twain's elemental imagination lends vigor and freshness to many passages. As Huck and Jim lie on their backs at night looking up at the stars, while the raft slips silently down the river, they argue about whether the stars "was made or only just happened": "Jim said the moon could 'a' *laid* them; well, that looked kind of reasonable . . . because I've seen a frog lay most as many." Huck describes Pap as having hair that was "long and tangled and greasy, and hung down, and you could see his eyes shining through like he was behind vines," while his face was white—"not like another man's white, but a white to make a body sick . . . a fish-belly white." At the parlor funeral of Peter Wilks, "the undertaker he slid around in his black gloves with his softy soothering ways, . . . making no more sound than a cat. . . . He was the softest, glidingest, stealthiest man I ever see." When the old king got a sudden shock, he "squshed down like a bluff bank that the river has cut under, it took him so sudden." Huck's language is equal to any effect demanded of it.

Part of the power of this book lies in Mark Twain's drawing of the character of Nigger Jim. From the time Jim first appears, a "big nigger" silhouetted in the kitchen door with the light behind him, he is a figure of dignity. In the famous syllogism in which Jim argues that since a Frenchman is a man, he should talk like a man, Mark Twain shows Jim's slow, purposeful reasoning. But in other moods Jim's spirit opens out to a wider horizon. Like Huck, he senses the beauty of the river. In his interpretation of a dream, Jim lets "the big, clear river" symbolize "the free States"—in other words, freedom. If "The Enchanted Village" might serve as a subtitle for *Tom Sawyer*, so "The Road to Freedom" might serve the same purpose for *Huckleberry Finn*. Jim has two big scenes in the book. One occurs when he relates the tragic moment of his discovery that his little girl was "plumb deef en dumb, Huck, plumb deef and dumb." His second big scene comes when he risks capture to help the doctor care for the wounded Tom Sawyer.

Whatever may be said of Tom Sawyer, Huck Finn is a developing character. Much of his development is due to his association with Jim and his increasing respect for the black man. In *Tom Sawyer*, Huck apologized to Tom for eating with a Negro, the Rogerses' Uncle Jake, who had given him food: "A body's got to do things when he's awful hungry he wouldn't . . . do as a steady thing." When he first finds Jim on the island, he is glad simply because he wants companionship; but as the two share the peace of the place, Huck comes to regard Jim as a human being rather than a faithful dog. When he hears there is a reward for Jim, the money offers no temptation to him; but under attack by his conscience, he fears he may have done wrong in helping a slave to escape. His traditions and environment pull him one way; what he feels in his heart pulls him the other way. Finally, he goes so far as to write a note to Miss Watson, Jim's owner, telling her where Jim is to be found. At first, he feels better for writing the note:

> . . . thinking how near I come to being lost and going to hell. . . . [Then I] got to thinking over our trip down the river; and I see Jim before me all the time: in the day and in the night-time, . . . and we a-floating along, talking and singing and laughing. But somehow I couldn't seem to strike no places to harden me against him, but only the other kind . . . and then I happened to look around and see that paper.
>
> It was a close place. I took it up and held it in my hand. I was a-trembling, because I'd got to decide, forever, betwixt two things, and I knowed it. I studied a minute, sort of holding my breath, and then says to myself:
>
> "All right, then, I'll *go* to hell"—and tore it up.

A part of Huck's development came when he apologized to Jim for fooling him about a dream. Jim very properly resented Huck's deceit, and Huck was abashed before Jim's stately indignation. When Huck waked in the night to find Jim mourning for his children—"Po' little 'Lizabeth! po' little Johnny!"—a new realization was borne in upon the boy: "I do believe he cared just as much for his people as white folks does for their'n. It don't seem natural, but I reckon it's so." Although the doctor and others seemed amazed at Jim's risking capture to aid the wounded Tom, Huck felt no surprise at all: "I knowed he was white inside."

The beautiful stretches of the river had power over Huck's spirit, as is shown in his own words: "It was kind of solemn, drifting down the big, still river . . . looking up at the stars, and we didn't ever feel like talking loud, and it warn't often we laughed." He has learned to read early in the story, and he reads at the Grangerford home; of *Pilgrim's Progress*, his verdict is, "The statements was interesting, but tough." He feels that somebody should write a poetical tribute to the dead Emmeline Grangerford, "so I tried to sweat out a verse or two myself, but I couldn't seem to make it go somehow." Such a sentiment would have seemed out of character for Huck in the beginning, but not now. He describes Colonel Grangerford as an aristocrat, and his own sensitive nature responds to the Colonel's fine-wire temperament: "everybody was always good-mannered where he was."

The first thematic unit ends with the smashing of the raft by a steamboat. This incident also ended the writing of *Huckleberry Finn* for almost seven years.[2] Mark Twain had written thus far in the summer of 1876; he apparently had no further plan, and when the raft was smashed, he stopped the book. Two years after he had shelved *Huckleberry Finn*, he wrote the 1878 letter to Howells, explaining that he felt himself unable to write successful satire because to do so calls for "a calm, judicial good humor." His trip down the river in 1882 to get material for *Life on the Mississippi* naturally recalled the river story to his mind. He must have then arrived at the design which made the book a masterpiece. All the meannesses of Mark Twain's "damned human race" are seen through the eyes and presented through the lips of Huck Finn. And thus Mark Twain was enabled, at last, to attain the calm detachment with which satire should be presented.

The second thematic unit begins when Huck stops at the Grangerford mansion after the wreck of the raft. The Grangerford-Shepherdson feud is one of the most tragic things in the book, but nothing is told with greater restraint. This restraint is art; but Mark Twain, as John Erskine observed, makes it seem the work of nature. Beginning his account of the climax of the feud, Huck says, "I don't want to talk much about the next day." All that blood and dying was nauseating to the boy, and "it would make him sick again" if he should tell about the killings. He tries not to remember the details, because those memories spoil his sleep at night. To measure Mark Twain's growth in artistry, one has only to compare this restraint with the early sketches in which the reformer purposefully emphasized blood and violence for their shock value in directing attention to situations he deplored. Now, to get back to the raft and to Jim is, for Huck, like going home; and his soul expands in the healing peace of the quiet river: "We said there warn't no home like a raft. . . . Other places do seem so cramped up and smothery."

After the episode of the feud, the king and the duke board the raft and begin to dominate the lives of Huck and Jim. The loafers of Bricksville, Arkansas, lean and whittle; around noon, they all laugh and look glad, for old man Boggs comes riding into town drunk and begins to blackguard Colonel Sherburn. Finally Sherburn's outraged honor demands that he stop blackguarding with a bullet, and Boggs dies in a little drugstore, with a heavy Bible on his chest.

All these wrongs are condemned through the mere fact of their presentation. With the exception of one scene, Mark Twain is invisible, inaudible, lost in the artistry of Huck's particular kind of communication. In that scene Colonel Sherburn appears on his veranda to pour his withering scorn down upon the mob and send them scurrying like whipped curs. "I know you clear through. I was born and raised in the South, and I've lived in the North." It is Mark Twain speaking:

So I know the average all around. The average man's a coward . . . Your mistake is that you didn't bring a man with you; that's one mistake, and the other is that you didn't come in the dark and fetch your masks. . . . The pitifulest thing out is a mob . . . But a mob without any *man* at the head of it is *beneath* pitifulness.

Now the thing for *you* to do is to droop your tails and go home and crawl in a hole.

Mark Twain's voice rings out, clear and unmistakable, in the hit at militarism: "an army is—a mob; they don't fight with courage that's born in them, but with courage that's borrowed from their mass." If a "Colonel" had talked like that, would Huck have reported him like that? No matter; the force of the book is so strong at this point that the illusion is not shattered; but the utter objectivity of the scene immediately preceding ranks it far above this one.

There, we see the innate cruelty of the dead-alive loafers. "There couldn't anything wake them up all over, and make them happy all over, like . . . putting turpentine on a stray dog and setting fire to him, or tying a tin pan to his tail and see him run himself to death." Then old Boggs rides in "on the waw-path," a pitiful figure who "throwed his hat down in the mud and rode over it, and . . . went a-raging down the street again, with his gray hair a-flying" while the loafers, at first "listening and laughing and going on," are quickly sobered by the ultimatum of Colonel Sherburn. "Everybody that seen the shooting was telling how it happened," and one "long, lanky man, with long hair and a big white fur stovepipe hat" enacted the scene in its entirety. Huck's comment is, "The people that had seen the thing said he done it perfect." And Mr. DeVoto adds that the long lanky man records this society "with an unemotional certainty beside which either Mr. Lewis's anger or Mr. Anderson's misery" seems merely hysterical. Those who understand Mark Twain can only guess how much of that calm detachment, that "unemotional certainty," was sheer artistry, a triumph of technique.

With each of these scenes, Huck's character develops as his experience is widened. He perceives the manly qualities of Jim and scales correctly the duke and the king; he knows that the duke is not so low as the king, and yet he is tolerant of the "poor old king" when he sees him in "a little low doggery, very tight, and a lot of loafers bullyragging him for sport." When Huck finds himself stranded on the *Walter Scott* with some murderers, his sympathy, broad and beautiful, makes him realize "how dreadful it was, even for murderers, to be in such a fix. I says to myself, there ain't no telling but I might come to be a murderer myself yet, and then how would I like it?" In his last glimpse of the king and the duke, tarred and feathered so that they "just looked like a couple of monstrous big soldier-plumes," he was "sorry for them poor pitiful rascals," and it made him sick to see it: "Human beings *can* be awful cruel to one another."

There is an occasional hint of determinism in *Huckleberry Finn*. Early in the story Huck backslides under the power of environment while living with Pap: ". . . I was used to being where I was, and liked it." If fear of his drunken father had not driven him forth, Mark Twain seems to say, Huck might have become another Pap. When his conscience troubles him over not giving up the runaway slave, he excuses himself on the ground of early environment and its effects:

> . . . .I knowed very well I had done wrong, and I see it warn't no use for me to try to learn to do right; a body that don't get *started* right when he's little ain't got no show—when the pinch comes there ain't nothing to back him up. . . . Then I . . . says to myself, hold on; s'pose you'd a done right and give Jim up, would you felt better than what you do now? No, I says, I'd feel bad—I'd feel just the same way I do now. Well, then, says I, what's the use you learning to do right when it's troublesome to do right and ain't no trouble to do wrong, and the wages is the same?

Huck's questioning of himself recalls Ernest Hemingway's definition of morality, which appears early in *Death in the Afternoon*: "I know only that what is moral is what you feel good after." Unquestionably, Mark Twain and Hemingway are akin in their preoccupation with death and in the care and skill with which they write the idiom of their people; but it seems to me that Hemingway's nearest approach to the earlier writer lies in the moral tests his characters apply inwardly. Having no moral code to go by, they test an action by the way they feel after it.[3]

Huck usually looks into his own heart for guidance. He "goes to studying things out" whenever he feels himself "in a tight place." He learns from experience, but his environment determines him only as his experiences develop what is within. Moral intuition is the basis on which his character rests. But if a man is not responsible to God or to society, and Mark Twain's determinism holds that he is not, why should he be responsible to himself? The inner voice of conscience, the voice of God, always holds him morally responsible. In this way *Huckleberry Finn* is a wise book, as all great books are wise.

· · ·

Huck wins his battle with his "yaller dog" conscience and continues, Mr. DeVoto observes, to vindicate "the realities of friendship, loyalty, and courage." DeVoto doubts that Mark Twain could have asserted them except in the belief of a boy. Perhaps it was, in part, the comparatively keen consciences of the young that attracted him. Like Hawthorne, he accepted the dramatic reality of the issues of conscience; Huck's conscience becomes the battleground for the chief struggle of the book. Although not dissatisfied with life, Huck is sometimes briefly pessimistic, as when he predicts that his Pap has likely "got [the money] all away from Judge Thatcher and drunk it up." But this prediction does not leave him despondent—he is ready to accept life as it comes. And Mr. DeVoto insists that "if the book makes a statement through Nigger Jim that human life is tragic, it also asserts through Huck that human life is noble . . . noble enough for the likes of us. . . . It is not a book of despair but rather of realistic acceptance."

It is chiefly in his boy-books, however, that Mark Twain was able to achieve this "realistic acceptance," this synthesis of both aspects of life. The joint charge of Brooks and DeVoto that he was imprisoned in his boyhood is thus seen to have supporting evidence. But the reason for that apparent imprisonment is also plain: Mark Twain was artist enough to know—or to sense, unconsciously, if you will—that such a synthesis, such a realistic acceptance, is demanded by the very nature of art. And so he turned again and again to the boy-world, the place where he could best achieve that synthesis and achieve it honestly. For he was honest; and he could rarely bring himself to an acceptance of human nature as exemplified in adults.

[1] I am indebted to Professor Floyd Stovall for the suggestion that *Huckleberry Finn* is a satire on institutionalism, as well as for some suggestions pertaining to the structure of the book.

[2] DeVoto, *Mark Twain at Work*, pp. 53, 62.

[3] Joseph Warren Beach said, "In certain ways, contemporary American fiction opens with Ernest Hemingway." In the first chapter of *Green Hills of Africa*, Hemingway himself said: "All modern American literature comes from one book by Mark Twain called *Huckleberry Finn.* . . . it's the best book we've had. All American writing comes from that. There was nothing before. There has been nothing as good since."

*The Unity and Coherence of *Huckleberry Finn*

The most obvious element of structure in *Huck Finn*, and the one most often noticed, is the picaresque journey down the river, full of inconsequently interspersed and apparently aimless adventures. But it is dangerous to say that much and stop, for the inconsequence does not preclude a plan, and the aimlessness is only apparent. Trilling, in discussing the special qualities of the river as a road, points out some profitable directions for further inquiry. The important thing, he says, is that the river is a moving road,

> . . . and the movement of the road in its own mysterious life transmutes the primitive simplicity of the form: the road itself is the greatest character in this novel of the road, and the hero's departures from the river and his returns to it compose a subtle and significant pattern. The linear simplicity of the picaresque novel is further modified by the story's having a clear dramatic organization: it has a beginning, a middle, and an end, and a mounting suspense of interest.[1]

Trilling perhaps oversimplifies the linear quality of the picaresque novel as Clemens knew it, but he does not overestimate the complexity of *Huck Finn*, and his observations on the "living" quality of the river and on the alternation of Huck's river and shore experiences are valuable clues.

Another clue, of perhaps even greater value, is furnished by James M. Cox's discussion of Huck's "initiation." According to Cox the "fake murder" that Huck stages in order to get away from his father "is probably the most vital and crucial incident of the entire novel,"[2] and Cox's observations on this event come close to defining the basic structure of the novel. The basic structure, which expresses the theme of the boy's growth and which carries the weight of the incidents and the imagery throughout, is a pattern of symbolic death and rebirth. As Cox points out, the central action on the river begins with Huck's pretended death. It ends with his mistaken recognition as Tom by Aunt Sally Phelps, when he feels that "it was like being born again, I was so glad to find out who I was." This pattern is kept in the focus of the reader's attention, as Cox also observes, by repeated deaths and escapes occurring between, before, and after the main events.

The pattern of death and rebirth is reinforced by the pattern Trilling observes in Huck's departures from and returns to the river; only we need to reverse Trilling's terms, for it is Huck's departures from and returns to shore which are cognate and parallel to the pattern of death and rebirth. The same pattern provides the framework for the "clear dramatic organization" which Trilling notices, and it roughly determines the kind of beginning,

*By Richard P. Adams, from *Tulane Studies in English*, VI (1956).

middle, and end that the story has. Putting Cox and Trilling together, and oversimplifying for the sake of initial clarity, we can state a more nearly complete definition of the structure of *Huckleberry Finn*. The beginning is Huck's life on shore in and around the village of St. Petersburg with the Widow Douglas and Pap. The middle, initiated by Huck's fake death, is his withdrawal from the life of society and civilization to the river; this withdrawal is repeated after each of his adventures on land. The end is his equivocal rebirth, his qualified return, under a false identity and with many reservations, to civilized life at the Phelps plantation.

The pattern of death and rebirth is also intimately concerned in the "mounting suspense of interest" which Trilling notes. The theme of the book, as we have hinted, is the same as that of *Tom Sawyer*: the growth of a boy to manhood, and his final acceptance of adult moral responsibilities. In this connection the pattern of death and rebirth is more than a technical device. In the tradition of romantic literature, to which *Huck Finn* belongs, it is a form with a meaning. The growth of a boy to manhood is perhaps the most popular of all themes for romantic fiction, and the structure which best expresses it is that of the death-and-rebirth pattern. The reason for this association is based in romantic philosophy, according to which the individual human personality is conceived as an organism, which cannot undergo a fundamental change of any kind without being totally reconstituted. Its old self "dies" and its new self, an unpredictably different organism, is "born." Huck's initiation, his transformation from boy to man, is such a change. It is a radical reconstitution of his moral attitude toward the society in which he lives. He grows, therefore, during the time of crucial change, by "dying" out of society, withdrawing into nature on the river, and then returning or being "reborn" into society with a new and different attitude toward it.

It should not have to be said that this return is by no means an uncritical acceptance of conventional social values. The process of Huck's moral growth is, in fact, most emphatically indicated by his decision, made on three separate but closely related occasions, to free Jim from slavery, which is an act of rebellion against society. In a superficial sense the three decisions are the same, but each means more than the one before, because Huck knows more about the society he is deciding to oppose and because he sees more fully and clearly the implications of the decision and its probable consequences.

The context, which becomes increasingly solid and massive as Huck's knowledge increases, is a complex interrelationship of social, cultural, political, and economic forces. We might skeletonize it by making three simple statements, which we can then elaborate. First, slavery is evil. Second, the pseudo-aristocratic society of the ante-bellum South which fosters and depends on slavery is also evil. Third, the sentimental cultural veneer with which that society conceals its evil from itself, if not from others, is evil as well. These propositions apply with increasing cogency to Huck's three

91

decisions, as he learns more about the character and workings, the concrete personal meanings and moral values, of Southern slave-holding aristocracy. The relations among these three intertwined thematic strands in *Huck Finn* are so complex and pervasive that a thorough explication of them would be longer than the book. I shall not try to exhaust them here, but rather to indicate their general character and, by exploring a few of them in some detail, to show how they work.

Huck's first decision to help Jim escape is made casually enough in the process of his own flight from civilization and from the domination of his father. When he comes across his fellow runaway on Jackson's Island, he is so glad to have his lonesomeness relieved by any sort of company that he hardly thinks of difficulties. " 'People would call me a low-down Abolitionist and despise me for keeping mum,' " he admits to Jim, " '—but that don't make no difference. I ain't a-going to tell, and I ain't a-going back there, anyways.' " But even this first and easiest decision is preceded by a fairly substantial development of motives and of symbolic motifs. Huck has been introduced to respectable society at the Widow's, where gentility is manifested painfully to him in regular hours, formal meals, and stiff clothing. When Miss Watson tells him about the bad place, he says he wishes he were there. "She got mad then, but I didn't mean no harm. All I wanted was to go somewheres. . . ." Later the same night, in harmony with the fake murder which is to come, he says, "I felt so lonesome I most wished I was dead." Then, in the planning and organization of Tom Sawyer's gang, we see Huck's indirect exposure to the culture of popular books and the sentimental proprieties of "high-toned" robbery and exploitation. Tom and the gang, of course, are completely unrealistic about the crimes they propose to commit, and blissfully unaware that crime, as gilded by the popular romances, is morally wrong. Farther on, Huck is regaled with Pap's reverse snobbishness on the subject of education and with his poor-white's groundless assertion of superiority over the much better educated "free nigger."

These lights and others like them are placed so as to reveal what Clemens considered to be the characteristic weaknesses, follies, and injustices of prewar Southern society. The essentially false and hypocritical gentility of the would-be aristocracy, the febrile and morally confusing sentimentalism of its favorite literature, and the crime of slavery which was the real basis of its economic and social system are continually brought home to Huck and the reader, in all kinds of dramatic, representative, and symbolic ways. The incidents are not haphazardly chosen or arranged. Each has its revealing gleam to contribute to Huck's unconsciously dawning awareness of the true values of the civilization to which he is being asked to belong. The result is that he runs away and, without any great misgivings at first, agrees to help Jim do the same.

The second decision is made necessary by a qualm of conscience. The fugitives are approaching Cairo, or think they are, and they both believe that Jim is almost free. Says Huck, "It hadn't ever come home to me before, what this thing was that I was doing. But now it did; and it stayed with me, and scorched me more and more." The point of difficulty is that freeing Jim involves robbing his owner, Miss Watson, of the eight hundred dollars he is worth on the market; and Jim makes the difficulty greater by threatening to have his children stolen, if necessary, by an Abolitionist. Huck is immediately and properly horrified. "It most froze me to hear such talk. . . . Here was this nigger, which I had as good as helped to run away, coming right out flat-footed and saying he would steal his children—children that belonged to a man I didn't even know; a man that hadn't ever done me no harm." The juxtaposition of "his" and "belonged" in this sentence, so carefully calculated to drive home the shocking injustice of property rights in human flesh, should not obscure the fact that there is a real moral issue. The great wrong of slavery does not make the lesser wrong of robbery right; a point which most pre-Civil War anti-slavery propagandists preferred to overlook. The issue is resolved by the fact that Huck finds hiimself unable to turn Jim in, for reasons which he does not fully understand but which the reader can surmise. To put it most simply, his human feelings are stronger than the commercial morality with which they are in conflict—as of course they should be. Unable to do entirely right, he chooses the lesser evil and goes on helping Jim.

When he repudiates his own conscience in this way, Huck takes a long step farther in his repudiation of Southern society, which has formed his conscience. He says to himself, in his usual innocent way, "what's the use you learning to do right when it's troublesome to do right and ain't no trouble to do wrong, and the wages is just the same? . . . So I reckoned I wouldn't bother no more about it, but after this always do whichever come handiest at the time." The innocence is of Huck, not Clemens, and it represents a remarkably keen penetration into the difficult question of personal or individual morality in relation to social conventions. Huck realizes in practice, though never in conscious theory, that the question is not one of a simple conflict between the individual and the mass, or the social institution, but that the two interpenetrate, and that the individual conscience is usually an ally of the social pressure for conformity.

Thoreau, in "Civil Disobedience," feels himself on solid ground when his conscience tells him to oppose the extension of slavery and the government that sanctions and promotes it. "If," he says, "the injustice . . . is of such a nature that it requires you to be the agent of injustice to another, then, I say, break the law." That seems comparatively easy; all that is needed is the courage to stand up against the government, which Southerners have always had in abundance. But, when the ante-bellum conscience is formed in Missouri instead of Massachusetts, the battle becomes intensely complicated. Its lines are drawn mostly inside the personality, which is then divided against itself. As Trilling remarks, it is the paradox in Huck's own thinking, by the terms of which he does right by doing what he thoroughly believes, in his conscious mind, to be wrong, that makes his character heroic and Clemens's satire brilliant.[3] His battle is desperate, his victory sublime. If it is fine to follow as Thoreau does the dictates of conscience over law, it is finer and much more difficult to follow those of the right over conscience and law combined.

• • •

The third and final decision is led up to by a more personal and extensive experience of upperclass Southerners than before. Shortly after the second crisis, Huck and Jim realize that they have passed Cairo in the fog, but before they can do anything to get back, the raft is wrecked by a steamboat and they are separated again. Huck finds himself ashore, beginning a new phase of the story and of his education. His shore adventures alternate, from this point on, with repeated escapes to the river, until he comes to the Phelps plantation. These adventures bring him more dramatically than before into contact, and more often into conflict, with aristocrats of various kinds. The increase of experience, knowledge, and understanding which he gains in this phase leads convincingly to his ultimate decision to repudiate aristocratic society by freeing its victim Jim.

The first aristocrats he meets in person, leaving aside the Widow, Miss Watson, and Judge Thatcher, are the Grangerfords, by whom he is strongly impressed and who are genuinely impressive in many ways. They have the typical aristocratic virtues: they are dignified, hospitable, proud, handsome, cultured (after a fashion), courteous, devout, and kind to strangers and dependents. But the more Huck learns of them, the more uneasy he becomes about their character and behavior. Clemens, through Huck's observations and comments, gradually undercuts the value of their culture. The description of the house, which is parallel to the account of "The House Beautiful" in *Life on the Mississippi*, is a skillful piece of irony. Huck admires the place immensely, while Clemens mercilessly exposes the queer mixture of arrogant show and pathetic provincialism that it presents to even a moderately sophisticated eye. The description leads up to and is ludicrously topped off by Huck's account of Emmeline Grangerford's esthetic misdeeds in crayon and verse, of the graveyard school run wild and gone to seed. The cultural pretensions of the aristocracy are, by this report, sufficiently harmless in themselves but crude, anachronistic, and highly absurd from any civilized modern point of view.

The feud which is going on between the Grangerfords and the Shepherdsons is a much more serious matter, and it does not depend on the same kind of irony for its effect. It is as deeply horrifying to Huck as it could possibly be to Clemens. The brutal killing of the two boys makes Huck so sick that he cannot even tell about it in detail without getting sick again; and his admiration for the better qualities of the aristocrats is more than canceled by this result of their violence.

The incident is a direct expression of feeling on the part of its author. In *Life on the Mississippi* Clemens goes somewhat out of his way to comment on a published opinion that the South had "the highest type of civilization this continent has seen . . ." He demonstrates the hollowness of the brag in a footnote with "Illustrations of it thoughtlessly omitted by the advertiser," consisting of newspaper accounts of four fights in which five Southern gentlemen were killed and one injured, with the usual incidental damage to bystanders, reference also being made to four other murders and one nonfatal stabbing in previous engagements involving some of the same gentlemen. The people concerned were of the highest class that Southern civilization had produced, including a general and his son, a bank president, a college professor, and "two 'highly connected' young Virginians" who fought a duel with butcher knives. It is from this kind of violence that Huck escapes to the river again, wishing that he "hadn't ever come ashore that night to see such things. I ain't ever going to get shut of them—lots of times I dream about them." Clemens had often dreamed about some violent episodes he witnessed as a boy.

Huck's reaction leads to one of his most lyric descriptions of the freedom, comfort, and beauty of the river, and the loveliness of life on a raft. But evil comes into this world also, in the shape of the two confidence men who palm themselves off as "the rightful Duke of Bridgewater" and "the late Dauphin . . . Looy the Seventeen, son of Looy the Sixteen and Marry Antonette," and who take over in the true aristocratic, robber-gang fashion. The cream of the jest is that the duke's claim is accepted by the other rogue so that he may in turn make his higher claim. The cream of the cream is that the duke then has to admit the king's superior status and rights in order that both may exploit the plebeian members of the little commonwealth. But the richest layer of all is Huck's good-naturedly cynical accommodation to the whole arrangement. He sees immediately what frauds these are, but he is pleased when the duke knuckles under; "for what you want, above all things, on a raft, is for everybody to be satisfied, and feel right and kind towards the others."

Clemens's feeling about the kind of imposition practiced—or at least attempted—here is given in a notebook entry: "There are shams and shams; there are frauds and frauds, but the transparentest of all is the sceptered one. We see monarchs meet and go through solemn ceremonies, farces, with straight countenances; but it is not possible to imagine them meeting in private and not laughing in each other's faces."[4] The fraud practiced by the bogus king and duke is no different from the frauds put over by real kings and dukes, except that the latter are bigger. As Huck explains to Jim, after the confidence men have worked over their first town together, they are lucky not to have Henry VIII on their hands, for he was a really accomplished crook; " 'If we'd 'a' had him along 'stead of our kings he'd 'a' fooled that town a heap worse than ourn done. I don't say that ourn is lambs, because they ain't, when you come right down to the cold facts; but they ain't nothing to *that* old ram, anyway.' " This observation reinforces the point already made, implicitly, that the Grangerfords and Shepherdsons, by their more serious imitation of aristocratic ways, are only presenting a more pernicious version of something which at best is a sham and a fraud.

Perhaps the most emphatic impression of the ugly side of Southern chivalry is given by the incident in which Huck witnesses the coldblooded murder of old Boggs by Colonel Sherburn. Boggs is a noisy but harmless fool, Sherburn a fine example of aristocratic pride—brave and intelligent in his own way, but narrow, selfish, inconsiderate, harsh, and brutal. It is, again, a sickening scene, and it is based on a murder that Clemens witnessed as a boy. But it may be that the importance of the incident for the satirical aspect of the book lies mainly in the character of the townspeople, who are by and large a degraded lot. "There couldn't anything wake them up all over," says Huck, "and make them happy all over, like a dog-fight—unless it might be putting turpentine on a stray dog and setting fire to him, or tying a tin pan to his tail and see him run himself to death." They try half-heartedly to get Boggs to stop his offensive yelling and go home, but they also perversely enjoy the shooting and the old man's death, the view of the body in the drug store window, and the reenactment of the murder by one of the onlookers. When they go to Sherburn's house with the announced intention of lynching him, he lectures them contemptuously and drives them off with a shotgun, which he does not have to fire.

His contempt seems justified, on the face of things. These are the same people who, after hooting the Shakespearean efforts of the king and the duke, prove ripe for the Royal Nonesuch hoax. The duke, in his estimate of them, agrees with Sherburn. He prints at the foot of his handbill "LADIES AND CHILDREN NOT ADMITTED," remarking, " 'There . . . if that line don't fetch them, I don't know Arkansaw!' " It does. But the deeper point is not explicitly stated here, or anywhere else in *Huck Finn*, nor is it fully understood, we may suppose, by either Sherburn or the duke. They see well enough that the people are ignorant, cowardly, and gullible; they do not see that the reason for that fact is the apparently opposite fact that an aristocracy is in power. Clemens, however, was aware of it and well convinced that poverty, both of the flesh and of the spirit, is the mirror image of aristocratic splendor and that universal cruelty is inevitably characteristic of any society divided into rigid classes with hereditary inequalities of function, privilege, and status.

This principle is explained more clearly in *A Connecticut Yankee*. The Yankee is shocked at the way poor peasants in Arthurian England rush out, heedless of right or justice, and help each other hang their neighbors in their lord's behalf, apparently unable "to see anything horrible about it." His comment is almost a direct reference to the satire in *Huck Finn*.

It reminded me of a time thirteen centuries away, when the "poor whites" of our South who were always despised and frequently insulted by the slave-lords around them, and who owed their base condition simply to the presence of slavery in their midst, were yet pusillanimously ready to side with the slave-lords in all political moves for the upholding and perpetuating of slavery, and did also finally shoulder their muskets and pour out their lives in an effort to prevent the destruction of that very institution which degraded them. And there was only one redeeming feature connected with that pitiful piece of history; and that was, that secretly the "poor white" did detest the slave-lord, and did feel his own shame.

The Yankee also remarks that "It is enough to make a body ashamed of his race to think of the sort of froth that has always occupied its thrones without shadow of right or reason," and what Clemens obviously means is that any respectable race would blow such froth to the moon before letting it settle into power.

Huck, whose background is about as purely poor-white as it could be, is given almost exactly the same words—"It was enough to make a body ashamed of the human race"—to describe his feelings about the next incident. The king and duke are having a fine run of initial success in playing their confidence game on the Wilks girls and most of their neighbors. It is a game that Huck perfectly understands, and he becomes so much ashamed of himself for being involved in it, though unwillingly, that he takes the risky measure of telling the truth in order to break it up. The most painful aspect of the affair applies directly to the theme of slavery, being the inhumanity of the fake aristocrats in the sale of the Wilks family slaves, "the two sons up the river to Memphis, and their mother down the river to Orleans." Huck says again that "it most made me down sick to see it. . . . I can't ever get it out of my memory, the sight of them poor miserable girls and niggers hanging around each other's necks and crying . . ." The reader is likely to recall, as Clemens must have done, that this is not something only fakers do; it is precisely what Miss Watson does in planning to sell Jim "down to Orleans"; the general truth is that, as the Connecticut Yankee remarks in another place, "a privileged class, an aristocracy, is but a band of slaveholders under another name." The function of the king and duke is to show this basic identity, and underscore its meaning. Are these two scoundrels the most absurd, unmitigated, bare-faced buffoons of wickedness imaginable? So, Clemens wishes us to feel and understand, are all aristocrats. Kings, dukes, pirates, robbers, confidence men, and slaveholders are the same, and all sorry. Anyone who respects them is a fool, anyone who fears them is a coward, and anyone who supports them or submits to them is a slave himself.

Huck is none of these things, though he is almost infinitely goodnatured and accommodating. He goes along with the king and duke as well and as long as he can, and he feels sorry for them when the mob escorts them out of town, in tar and feathers, on a rail. But he spoils their game with the

Wilkses, and he leaves them when the king sells Jim into bondage again. For him, their function has been to complete his education in the social realities of slavocracy and to put the finishing touches on his preparation for the final decision he has to make. They have done the job effecitvely; he is ready now to see Jim through to freedom in spite of anything. Unconsciously, but with deep conviction, he understands the society to which by accident of birth he belongs, and refuses to submit to it.

On this last occasion, Huck sees his problem as being more difficult than it has ever seemed to him before, because it presents itself to him in terms of the religious sanction which the institution of slavery enjoyed in the prewar South. His conscience, unable to win the battle alone, now tells him, in accordance with the Sunday-school teaching he feels he should have had, " 'that people that acts as I'd been acting about that nigger goes to everlasting fire.' " Again, Huck is expressing one of his author's ideas. Clemens remarks of his mother in the *Autobiography* that,

> kind-hearted and compassionate as she was, I think she was not conscious that slavery was a bald, grotesque, and unwarrantable usurpation. She had never heard it assailed in any pulpit, but had heard it defended and sanctified in a thousand; her ears were familiar with Bible texts that approved it, but if there were any that disapproved it they had not been quoted by her pastors; as far as her experience went, the wise and the good and the holy were unanimous in the conviction that slavery was right, righteous, sacred, the peculiar pet of the Deity, and a condition which the slave himself ought to be daily and nightly thankful for.[5]

Huck has easily won out over public opinion, less easily over public opinion reinforced by his own conscience. The addition of the Deity to the list of powers with which he has to contend raises his battle to its ultimate pitch of intensity.

His first maneuver is to pray for the improvement of his character, but he realizes at once that the plea is hypocritical. To make it good, he writes a letter to Miss Watson to tell her where Jim is, but he gets to thinking about Jim's goodness and loyalty and kindness, and all the times they have helped each other, and again he makes up his mind.

> I was a-trembling, because I'd got to decide, forever, betwixt two things, and I knowed it. I studied a minute, sort of holding my breath, and then says to myself:
> "All right, then, I'll *go* to hell"—and tore it up.
> It was awful thoughts and awful words, but they was said. And I let them stay said; and never thought no more about reforming.

With this decision, the middle or river section comes to its conclusion, and the ending of the book begins.

Clemens obviously had difficulty handling the ending. The reason seems to be that once Huck's final decision is made there is no longer any important part for Jim to play. His function in relation to the theme has been to test, or to furnish occasions when events would test, Huck's growing moral strength and mature independence. When that has been done, to the last possible extreme, Jim needs simply to be got out of the book as quickly and as unobtrusively as possible. Instead, Clemens plays up Tom Sawyer's long, elaborate, and almost meaningless escape plot. The final solution to the problem, the disclosure that Miss Watson has died and freed Jim in her will, is all that is needed, and the less said about it the better. And yet the escape plot is not altogether irrelevant. It furthers and completes the satire on sentimental literature, from which Tom draws his inspirations. It caps the ridicule of aristocratic pretensions by identifying Jim, the imprisoned slave, with the noble persons on whose renowned adventures his liberation is modeled. It is an immense expression of contempt for adult society, so easily and so thoroughly hoodwinked by a pair of audacious children; and the more absurd Tom's antics become, the more the satire is built up. It is as much an attack on conventional respectability as Huck's discomforts at the Widow Douglas's or his observations on the culture of the Grangerfords, or his rebellion against slavery itself.

Huck's attitude at the end is a mixture, full of ironies and reservations of many kinds. Having made the great decision to repudiate society, physically, morally, and spiritually, he can hardly return to it without equivocation. In a sense, his acceptance of the name and status of Tom Sawyer on the Phelps plantation is a return, but it is made on completely false premises. Also Huck is glad in a way to submit to Tom's leadership and direction. The burden of lonely responsibility has weighed long and heavily. But he is not fooled for a minute into thinking that there is any validity in Tom's adherence to bookish or aristocratic authority. " 'When I start in to steal a nigger,' " he says, " 'I ain't no ways particular how it's done so it's done. What I want is my nigger . . . and I don't give a dead rat what the authorities thinks about it nuther.' " He has arrived at maturity and self-sufficiency, and he is poised at the end in a delicate balance, ready at any moment "to light out for the territory" in order to escape Aunt Sally's threatened continuation of the civilizing process begun by the Widow Douglas.

This aspect of the conclusion is exactly right. It would have been wrong—impossible in fact—for Clemens to bring the story to a stop, as he might have tried to do by having Huck accept the moral values of society and return to it uncritically in a "happy ending." The whole process of his development runs counter to any such result. The impression that Clemens has to leave, and does leave, in the reader's mind and feelings is that Huck will continue to develop. He will escape again, as many times as he needs to, from society and any of its restrictions which would hamper or prevent his growth. He will die and be reborn whenever his character needs to break the mold that society would place upon it. Accordingly, the structure of the story is left open; the conclusion is deliberately inconclusive.

Frank Baldanza, who has made the most direct attack so far on the problem of structure in *Huck Finn*, believes that the basic principle can be defined as rhythmic repetition, with variation and development, of many thematic motifs, which have the effect of stitching the book together internally. He further suggests that each recurrence "was impulsive on Twain's part, and that any pattern we find in the repetitions is either unconsciously or accidentally ordained."[6] My analysis would seem to bear out the observation that rhythmic, varied, and developmental repetition is important. It is not basic to the structure, but it certainly does support it and supply it with a texture of rich and complex harmony. However, this effect is not and cannot possibly be accidental; it fits too well with the larger thematic repetition of Huck's decision. And I suspect very strongly too that Clemens must have been aware of it, in some way, as being appropriate to the pattern of the work he meant to make. A close examination will show that the motifs most often repeated are those most intimately concerned with the aristocracy-slavery-sentimentalism relationship. Moreover the variations add up to a steady intensification of Huck's and the reader's awareness of the injustice, the hypocrisy, and the general moral ugliness and weakness of the injustice, the hypocrisy, and the general moral ugliness and weakness of Southern society before the war. This intensification provides the milieu and the measure of Huck's development through the death-and-rebirth pattern from irresponsible boyhood to moral maturity.

The total result of these thematic, structural, and symbolic workings is a novel which has a remarkably high degree of consistency, coherence, and unity. Its theme is the growth of an individual personality. Its crisis is the moral decision, repeated three times, to repudiate the conventions of society and do the individually, humanly right thing. Its rising interest is given by the sharply increasing complexity of the individual awareness of the implications of such an action. Its structure is defined by the extinction of the old childish organization of mind and feelings, the symbolic death of the individual as he was, his withdrawal from society into nature, and his reconstitution, or symbolic rebirth, on a higher and more mature level of organization, as a better, more capable person. The theme and structure are concretely embodied and related in the texture, which reinforces both with a rhythmically repeated and varied pattern of appropriate motifs and images. The functional, organic interrelations of all these factors must have something to do with the effect of unity which readers generally feel in *Huckleberry Finn*, but which we are now only beginning to understand and be able to explain.

[1] Lionel Trilling, Introduction to the Rinehart edition of *The Adventures of Huckleberry Finn*, reprinted in *The Liberal Imagination* (New York, 1950), p. 115.

[2] James M. Cox, "Remarks on the Sad Initiation of Huckleberry Finn," *Sewanee Review*, LXII (1954), 395.

[3] Trilling, pp. 111-12.

[4] *Mark Twain's Notebook*, ed. A. B. Paine (New York and London, 1935), p. 196. Clemens neglected this view when he later met some royal persons himself.

[5] *Mark Twain's Autobiography*, ed. A. B. Paine (New York and London, 1924), I, 123.

[6] Frank Baldanza, "The Structure of *Huckleberry Finn*," *American Literature*, XXVII (November, 1955), 353.

*Mr. Eliot, Mr. Trilling, and *Huckleberry Finn*

> *In the losing battle that the plot fights with the characters, it often takes a cowardly revenge. Nearly all novels are feeble at the end. This is because the plot requires to be wound up. Why is this necessary? Why is there not a convention which allows a novelist to stop as soon as he feels muddled or bored? Alas, he has to round things off, and usually the characters go dead while he is at work, and our final impression of them is through deadness.*
>
> —E. M. FORSTER

The Adventures of Huckleberry Finn has not always occupied its present high place in the canon of American literature. When it was first published in 1885, the book disturbed and offended many reviewers, particularly spokesmen for the genteel tradition.[1] In fact, a fairly accurate inventory of the narrow standards of such critics might be made simply by listing epithets they applied to Clemens' novel. They called it vulgar, rough, inelegant, irreverent, coarse, semi-obscene, trashy and vicious.[2] So much for them. Today (we like to think) we know the true worth of the book. Everyone now agrees that *Huckleberry Finn* is a masterpiece: it is probably the one book in our literature about which highbrows and lowbrows can agree. Our most serious critics praise it. Nevertheless, a close look at what two of the best among them have recently written will likewise reveal, I believe, serious weaknesses in current criticism. Today the problem of evaluating the book is as much obscured by unqualified praise as it once was by parochial hostility.

I have in mind essays by Lionel Trilling and T. S. Eliot.[3] Both praise the book but in praising it both feel obligated to say something in justification of what so many readers have felt to be its great flaw: the disappointing "ending," the episode which begins when Huck arrives at the Phelps place and Tom Sawyer reappears. There are good reasons why Mr. Trilling and Mr. Eliot should feel the need to face this issue. From the point of view of scope alone, more is involved than the mere "ending"; the episode comprises almost one-fifth of the text. The problem, in any case, is unavoidable. I have discussed *Huckleberry Finn* in courses with hundreds of college students, and I have found only a handful who did not confess their dissatisfaction with the extravagant mock rescue of Nigger Jim and the denouement itself. The same question always comes up: "What went wrong with Twain's novel?" Even Bernard DeVoto, whose wholehearted commitment to Clemens' genius is well known, has said of the ending that "in the whole reach of the English novel there is no more abrupt or more

*By Leo Marx. From *The American Scholar*, XXII (Autumn, 1953).

chilling descent.''[4] Mr. Trilling and Mr. Eliot do not agree. They both attempt, and on similar grounds, to explain and defend the conclusion.

Of the two, Mr. Trilling makes the more moderate claim for Clemens' novel. He does admit that there is a "falling off" at the end; nevertheless he supports the episode as having "a certain formal aptness." Mr. Eliot's approval is without serious qualification. He allows no objections, asserts that "it is right that the mood of the end of the book should bring us back to the beginning." I mean later to discuss their views in some detail, but here it is only necessary to note that both critics see the problem as one of form. AND SO IT IS. Like many questions of form in literature, however, this one is not finally separable from a question of "content," of value, or, if you will, of moral insight. To bring *Huckleberry Finn* to a satisfactory close, Clemens had to do more than find a neat device for ending a story. His problem, though it may never have occurred to him, was to invent an action capable of placing in focus the meaning of the journey down the Mississippi.

I believe that the ending of *Huckleberry Finn* makes so many readers uneasy because they rightly sense that it jeopardizes the significance of the entire novel. To take seriously what happens at the Phelps farm is to take lightly the entire downstream journey. What is the meaning of the journey? With this question all discussion of *Huckleberry Finn* must begin. It is true that the voyage down the river has many aspects of a boy's idyl. We owe much of its hold upon our imagination to the enchanting image of the raft's unhurried drift with the current. The leisure, the absence of constraint, the beauty of the river—all these things delight us. "It's lovely to live on a raft." And the multitudinous life of the great valley we see through Huck's eyes has a fascination of its own. Then, of course, there is humor—laughter so spontaneous, so free of the bitterness present almost everywhere in American humor that readers often forget how grim a spectacle of human existence Huck contemplates. Humor in this novel flows from a bright joy of life as remote from our world as living on a raft.

Yet along with the idyllic and the epical and the funny in *Huckleberry Finn*, there is a coil of meaning which does for the disparate elements of the novel what a spring does for a watch. The meaning is not in the least obscure. It is made explicit again and again. The very words with which Clemens launches Huck and Jim upon their voyage indicate that theirs is not a boy's lark but a quest for freedom. From the electrifying moment when Huck comes back to Jackson's Island and rouses Jim with the news that a search party is on the way, we are meant to believe that Huck is enlisted in the cause of freedom. "Git up and hump yourself, Jim!" he cries. "There ain't a minute to lose. They're after us!" What particularly counts here is the *us*. No one is after Huck; no one but Jim knows he is alive. In that small word Clemens compresses the exhilarating power of Huck's instinctive humanity. His unpremeditated identification with Jim's flight from slavery is an unforgettable moment in American experience, and it may be said at once that any culmination of the journey which detracts from the urgency and dignity with which it begins will necessarily be unsatisfactory. Huck realizes this himself, and says so when, much later, he comes back to the raft after discovering that the Duke and the King have sold Jim:

> After all this long journey . . . here it was all come to nothing, everything all busted up and ruined, because they could have the heart to serve Jim such a trick as that, and make him a slave again all his life, and amongst strangers, too, for forty dirty dollars.

Huck knows that the journey will have been a failure unless it takes Jim to freedom. It is true that we do discover, in the end, that Jim is free, but we also find out that the journey was not the means by which he finally reached freedom.

The most obvious thing wrong with the ending, then, is the flimsy contrivance by which Clemens frees Jim. In the end we not only discover that Jim has been a free man for two months, but that his freedom has been granted by old Miss Watson. If this were only a mechanical device for terminating the action, it might not call for much comment. But it is more than that: it is a significant clue to the importance of the last ten chapters. Remember who Miss Watson is. She is the Widow's sister whom Huck introduces in the first pages of the novel. It is she who keeps ''pecking'' at Huck, who tries to teach him to spell and to pray and to keep his feet off the furniture. She is an ardent proselytizer for piety and good manners, and her greed provides the occasion for the journey in the first place. She is Jim's owner, and he decides to flee only when he realizes that she is about to break her word (she cannot resist a slave trader's offer of eight hundred dollars) and sell him down the river away from his family.

Miss Watson, in short, is the Enemy. If we except a predilection for physical violence, she exhibits all the outstanding traits of the valley society. She pronounces the polite lies of civilization that suffocate Huck's Spirit. The freedom which Jim seeks, and which Huck and Jim temporarily enjoy aboard the raft, is accordingly freedom *from* everything for which Miss Watson stands. Indeed, the very intensity of the novel derives from the discordance between the aspirations of the fugitives and the respectable code for which she is a spokesman. Therefore, her regeneration, of which the deathbed freeing of Jim is the unconvincing sign, hints a resolution of the novel's essential conflict. Perhaps because this device most transparently reveals that shift in point of view which he could not avoid, and which is less easily discerned elsewhere in the concluding chapters, Clemens plays it down. He makes little attempt to account for Miss Watson's change of heart, a change particularly surprising in view of Jim's brazen escape. Had Clemens given this episode dramatic emphasis appropriate to its function, Miss Watson's bestowal of freedom upon Jim would have proclaimed what the rest of the ending actually accomplishes—a vindication of persons and attitudes Huck and Jim had symbolically repudiated when they set forth downstream.

It may be said, and with some justice, that a reading of the ending as a virtual reversal of meanings implicit in the rest of the novel misses the point—that I have taken the final episode too seriously. I agree that Clemens certainly did not intend us to read it so solemnly. The ending, one might contend, is simply a burlesque upon Tom's taste for literary romance. Surely the tone of the episode is familiar to readers of Mark Twain. The preposterous monkey business attendant upon Jim's "rescue," the careless improvisation, the nonchalant disregard for common-sense plausibility—all these things should not surprise readers of Twain or any low comedy in the tradition of "Western humor." However, the trouble is, first, that the ending hardly comes off as burlesque: it is *too* fanciful, *too* extravagant; and it is tedious. For example, to provide a "gaudy" atmosphere for the escape, Huck and Tom catch a couple of dozen snakes. Then the snakes escape.

> No, there warn't no real scarcity of snakes about the house for a considerable spell. You'd see them dripping from the rafters and places every now and then; and they generly landed in your plate, or down the back of your neck . . .

Even if this were *good* burlesque, which it is not, what is it doing here? It is out of keeping; the slapstick tone jars with the underlying seriousness of the voyage.

Huckleberry Finn is a masterpiece because it brings Western humor to perfection and yet transcends the narrow limits of its conventions. But the ending does not. During the final extravaganza we are forced to put aside many of the mature emotions evoked earlier by the vivid rendering of Jim's fear of capture, the tenderness of Huck's and Jim's regard for each other, and Huck's excruciating moments of wavering between honesty and respectability. None of these emotions are called forth by the anticlimactic final sequence. I do not mean to suggest that the inclusion of low comedy per se is a flaw in *Huckleberry Finn*. One does not object to the shenanigans of the rogues; there is ample precedent for the place of extravagant humor even in works of high seriousness. But here the case differs from most which come to mind: the major characters themselves are forced to play low comedy roles. Moreover, the most serious motive in the novel, Jim's yearning for freedom, is made the object of nonsense. The conclusion, in short, is farce, but the rest of the novel is not.

That Clemens reverts in the end to the conventional manner of Western low comedy is most evident in what happens to the principals. Huck and Jim become comic characters; that is a much more serious ground for dissatisfaction that the unexplained regeneration of Miss Watson. Remember that Huck has grown in stature throughout the journey. By the time he arrives at the Phelps place, he is not the boy who had been playing robbers with Tom's gang in St. Petersburg the summer before. All he had seen and felt since he parted from Tom had deepened his knowledge of human nature and of himself. Clemens makes a point of Huck's development in two scenes which occur just before he meets Tom again. The first describes Huck's final capitulation to his own sense of right and wrong: "All right, then, I'll go to Hell." This is the climactic moment in the ripening of his selfknowledge. Shortly afterward, when he comes upon a mob riding the Duke and the King out of town on a rail, we are given his most memorable insight into the nature of man. Although these rogues had subjected Huck to every indignity, what he sees provokes this celebrated comment:

> Well, it made me sick to see it; and I was sorry for them poor pitiful rascals, it seemed like I couldn't ever feel any hardness against them any more in the world. It was a dreadful thing to see. Human beings *can* be awful cruel to one another.

The sign of Huck's maturity here is neither the compassion nor the skepticism, for both had been marks of his personality from the first. Rather, the special quality of these reflections is the extraordinary combination of the two, a mature blending of his instinctive suspicion of human motives with his capacity for pity.

But at this point Tom reappears. Soon Huck has fallen almost completely under his sway once more, and we are asked to believe that the boy who felt pity for the rogues is now capable of making Jim's capture the occasion for a game. He becomes Tom's helpless accomplice, submissive and gullible. No wonder that Clemens has Huck remark, when Huck first realizes Aunt Sally has mistaken him for Tom, that "it was like being born again." Exactly. In the end, Huck regresses to the subordinate role in which he had first appeared in *The Adventures of Tom Sawyer*. Most of those traits which made him so appealing a hero now disappear. He had never, for example, found pain or misfortune amusing. At the circus, when a clown disguised as a drunk took a precarious ride on a prancing horse, the crowd loved the excitement and danger; "it warn't funny to me, though," said Huck. But now, in the end, he submits in awe to Tom's notion of what is amusing. To satisfy Tom's hunger for adventure he makes himself a party to sport which aggravates Jim's misery.

It should be added at once that Jim doesn't mind too much. The fact is that he has undergone a similar transformation. On the raft he was an individual, man enough to denounce Huck when Huck made him the victim of a practical joke. In the closing episode, however, we lose sight of Jim in the maze of farcical invention. He ceases to be a man. He allows Huck and "Mars Tom" to fill his hut with rats and snakes, "and every time a rat bit Jim he would get up and write a line in his journal whilst the ink was fresh." This creature who bleeds ink and feels no pain is something less than human. He has been made over in the image of a flat stereotype: the submissive stage-Negro. These antics divest Jim, as well as Huck, of much of his dignity and individuality.[5]

What I have been saying is that the flimsy devices of plot, the discordant farcical tone, and the disintegration of the major characters all betray the failure of the ending. These are not aspects merely of form in a technical sense, but of meaning. For that matter, I would maintain that this book has little or no formal unity independent of the joint purpose of Huck and Jim. What components of the novel, we may ask, provide the continuity which links one adventure with another? The most important is the unifying consciousness of Huck, the narrator, and the fact that we follow the same principals through the entire string of adventures. Events, moreover, occur in a temporal sequence. Then there is the river; after each adventure Huck and Jim return to the raft and the river. Both Mr. Trilling and Mr. Eliot speak eloquently of the river as a source of unity, and they refer to the river as a god. Mr. Trilling says that Huck is "the servant of the river-god." Mr. Eliot puts it this way: "The River gives the books its form. But for the River, the book might be only a sequence of adventures with a happy ending." This seems to me an extravagant view of the function of the neutral agency of the river. Clemens has a knowledgeable respect for the Mississippi, and, without sanctifying it, was able to provide excellent reasons for Huck's and Jim's intense relation with it. It is a source of food and beauty and terror and serenity of mind. But above all, it provides motion; it is the means by which Huck and Jim move away from a menacing civilization. They return to the river to continue their journey. The river cannot, does not, supply purpose. That purpose is a facet of their consciousness, and without the motive of escape from society, *Huckleberry Finn* would indeed "be only a sequence of adventures." Mr. Eliot's remark indicates how lightly he takes the quest for freedom. His somewhat fanciful exaggeration of the river's role is of a piece with his neglect of the theme at the novel's center.

That theme is heightened by the juxtaposition of sharp images of contrasting social orders: the microcosmic community Huck and Jim establish aboard the raft and the actual society which exists along the Mississippi's banks. The two are separated by the river, the road to freedom upon which Huck and Jim must travel. Huck tells us what the river means to them when, after the Wilks episode, he and Jim once again shove their raft into the current: "It *did* seem so good to be free again and all by ourselves on the big river, and nobody to bother us." The river is indifferent. But its sphere is relatively uncontaminated by the civilization they flee, and so the river allows Huck and Jim some measure of freedom at once, the moment they set foot on Jackson's Island or the raft. Only on the island and the raft do they have a chance to practice that idea of brotherhood to which they are devoted. "Other places do seem so cramped up and smothery," Huck explains, "but a raft don't. You feel mighty free and easy and comfortable on a raft." The main thing is freedom.

On the raft the escaped slave and the white boy try to practice their code: "What you want, above all things, on a raft, is for everybody to be satisfied, and feel right and kind towards the others." This human credo constitutes the paramount affirmation of *The Adventures of Huckleberry Finn*, and it obliquely aims a devastating criticism at the existing social order. It is a creed which Huck and Jim bring to the river. It neither emanates from nature nor is it addressed to nature. Therefore I do not see that it means much to talk about the river as a god in this novel. The river's connection with this high aspiration for man is that it provides a means of escape, a place where the code can be tested. The truly profound meanings of the novel are generated by the impingement of the actual world of slavery, feuds, lynching, murder, and a spurious Christian morality upon the ideal of the raft. The result is a tension which somehow demands release in the novel's ending.

But Clemens was unable to effect this release and at the same time control the central theme. The unhappy truth about the ending of *Huckleberry Finn* is that the author, having revealed the tawdry nature of the culture of the great valley, yielded to its essential complacency. The general tenor of the closing scenes, to which the token regeneration of Miss Watson is merely one superficial clue, amounts to just that. In fact, this entire reading of *Huckleberry Finn* merely confirms the brilliant insight of George Santayana, who many years ago spoke of American humorists, of whom he considered Mark Twain an outstanding representative, as having only "half escaped" the genteel tradition. Santayana meant that men like Clemens were able to "point to what contradicts it in the facts; but not in order to abandon the genteel tradition, for they have nothing solid to put in its place." This seems to me the real key to the failure of *Huckleberry Finn*. Clemens had presented the contrast between the two social orders but could not, or would not, accept the tragic fact that the one he had rejected was an image of solid reality and the other an ecstatic dream. Instead he gives us the cozy reunion with Aunt Polly in a scene fairly bursting with approbation of the entire family, the Phelpses included.

Like Miss Watson, the Phelpses are almost perfect specimens of the dominant culture. They are kind to their friends and relatives; they have no taste for violence; they are people capable of devoting themselves to their spectacular dinners while they keep Jim locked in the little hut down by the ash hopper, with its lone window boarded up. (Of course Aunt Sally visits Jim to see if he is "comfortable," and Uncle Silas comes in "to pray with him.") These people with their comfortable Sunday-dinner conviviality and the runaway slave padlocked nearby, are reminiscent of those solid German citizens we have heard about in our time who tried to maintain a similarly *gemütlich* way of life within virtual earshot of Buchenwald. I do not mean to imply that Clemens was unaware of the shabby morality of such people. After the abortive escape of Jim, when Tom asks about him, Aunt Sally replies: "Him? . . . the runaway nigger? . . . They've got him back, safe and sound, and he's in the cabin again, on bread and water, and loaded down with chains, till he's claimed or sold!'' Clemens understood people like the Phelpses, but nevertheless he was forced to rely upon them to provide his happy ending. The satisfactory outcome of Jim's quest for freedom must be attributed to the benevolence of the very people whose inhumanity first made it necessary.

But to return to the contention of Mr. Trilling and Mr. Eliot that the ending is more or less satisfactory after all. As I have said, Mr. Trilling approves of the "formal aptness" of the conclusion. He says that "some device is needed to permit Huck to return to his anonymity, to give up the role of hero,'' and that therefore, "nothing could serve better than the mind of Tom Sawyer with its literary furnishings, its conscious romantic desire for experience and the hero's part, and its ingenious schematization of life. . . .'' Though more detailed, this is essentially akin to Mr. Eliot's blunt assertion that "it is right that the mood at the end of the book should bring us back to that of the beginning.'' I submit that it is wrong for the end of the book to bring us back to that mood. The mood of the beginning of *Huckleberry Finn* is the mood of Huck's attempt to accommodate himself to the ways of St. Petersburg. It is the mood of the end of *The Adventures of Tom Sawyer,* when the boys had been acclaimed heroes, and when Huck was accepted as a candidate for respectability. That is the state in which we find him at the beginning of *Huckleberry Finn.* But Huck cannot stand the new way of life, and his mood gradually shifts to the mood of rebellion which dominates the novel until he meets Tom again. At first, in the second chapter, we see him still eager to be accepted by the nice boys of the town. Tom leads the gang in re-enacting adventures he has culled from books, but gradually Huck's pragmatic turn of mind gets him in trouble. He has little tolerance for Tom's brand of make-believe. He irritates Tom. Tom calls him a "numbskull,'' and finally Huck throws up the whole business:

> So then I judged that all that stuff was only just one of Tom
> Sawyer's lies. I reckoned he believed in the A-rabs and the ele-
> phants, but as for me I think different. It had all the marks of a
> Sunday-school.

With this statement, which ends the third chapter, Huck parts company with Tom. The fact is that Huck has rejected Tom's romanticizing of experience; moreover, he has rejected it as part of the larger pattern of society's make-believe, typified by Sunday school. But if he cannot accept Tom's harmless fantasies about the A-rabs, how are we to believe that a year later Huck is capable of awe-struck submission to the far more extravagant fantasies with which Tom invests the mock rescue of Jim?

After Huck's escape from his "pap,'' the drift of the action, like that of the Mississippi's current, is *away* from St. Petersburg. Huck leaves Tom and the A-rabs behind, along with the Widow, Miss Watson, and all the pseudo-religious ritual in which nice boys must partake. The return, in the end, to the mood of the beginning therefore means defeat—Huck's defeat; to return to that mood *joyously* is to portray defeat in the guise of victory.

Mr. Eliot and Mr. Trilling deny this. The overriding consideration for them is form—form which seems largely to mean symmetry of structure. It is fitting, Mr. Eliot maintains, that the book should come full circle and bring Huck once more under Tom's sway. Why? Because it begins that way. But it seems to me that such structural unity is *imposed* upon the novel, and thefore is meretricious. It is a jerry-built structure, achieved only by sacrifice of characters and theme. Here the controlling principle of form apparently is unity, but unfortunately a unity much too superficially conceived. Structure, after all, is only one element—indeed, one of the more mechanical elements—of unity. A unified work must surely manifest coherence of meaning and clear development of theme, yet the ending of *Huckleberry Finn* blurs both. The eagerness of Mr. Eliot and Mr. Trilling to justify the ending is symptomatic of that absolutist impulse of our critics to find reasons, once a work has been admitted to the highest canon of literary reputability, for admiring every bit of it.

What is perhaps most striking about these judgments of Mr. Eliot's and Mr. Trilling's is that they are so patently out of harmony with the basic standards of both critics. For one thing, both men hold far more complex ideas of the nature of literary unity than their comments upon *Huckleberry Finn* would suggest. For another, both critics are essentially moralists, yet here we find them turning away from a moral issue in order to priase a dubious structural unity. Their efforts to explain away the flaw in Clemens' novel suffer from a certain narrowness surprising to anyone who knows their work. These facts suggest that we may be in the presence of a tendency in contemporary criticism which the critics themselves do not fully recognize.

Is there an explanation? How does it happen that two of our most respected critics should seem to treat so lightly the glaring lapse of moral imagination in *Huckleberry Finn*? Perhaps—and I stress the conjectural nature of what I am saying—perhaps the kind of moral issue raised by *Huckleberry Finn* is not the kind of moral issue to which today's criticism readily addressed itself. Today our critics, no less than our novelists and poets, are most sensitively attuned to moral problems which arise in the sphere of individual behavior. They are deeply aware of sin, of individual infractions of our culture's Christian ethic. But my impression is that they are, possibly because of the strength of the reaction against the mechanical sociological criticism of the thirties, less sensitive to questions of what might be called social or political morality.

By social or political morality I refer to the values implicit in a social system, values which may be quite distinct from the personal morality of any given individual within the society. Now *The Adventures of Huckleberry Finn*, like all novels, deals with the behavior of individuals. But one mark of Clemens' greatness is his deft presentation of the disparity between what people do when they behave as individuals and what they do when forced into roles imposed upon them by society. Take, for example, Aunt Sally and Uncle Silas Phelps, who consider themselves Christians, who are by impulse generous and humane, but who happen also to be staunch upholders of certain degrading and inhuman social institutions. When they are confronted with an escaped slave, the imperatives of social morality outweigh all pious professions.

The conflict between what people think they stand for and what social pressure forces them to do is central to the novel. It is present to the mind of Huck and, indeed, accounts for his most serious inner conflicts. He knows how he feels about Jim, but he also knows what he is expected to do about Jim. This division within his mind corresponds to the division of the novel's moral terrain into the areas represented by the raft on the one hand and society on the other. His victory over his "yaller dog" conscience therefore assumes heroic size: it is a victory over the prevailing morality. But the last fifth of the novel has the effect of diminishing the importance and uniqueness of Huck's victory. We are asked to assume that somehow freedom can be achieved in spite of the crippling power of what I have called the social morality. Consequently the less importance we attach to that force as it operates in the novel, the more acceptable the ending becomes.

Moreover, the idea of freedom, which Mr. Eliot and Mr. Trilling seem to slight, takes on its full significance only when we acknowledge the power which society exerts over the minds of men in the world of *Huckleberry Finn*. For freedom in this book specifically means freedom from society and its imperatives. This is not the traditional Christian conception of freedom. Huck and Jim seek freedom not from a burden of individual guilt and sin, but from social constraint. That is to say, evil in *Huckleberry Finn* is the product of civilization, and if this is indicative of Clemens' rather too simple view of human nature, nevertheless the fact is that Huck, when he can divest himself of the strain of social conditioning (as in the incantatory account of sunrise on the river), is entirely free of anxiety and guilt. The only guilt he actually knows arises from infractions of a social code. (The guilt he feels after playing the prank on Jim stems from his betrayal of the law of the raft.) Huck's and Jim's creed is secular. Its object is harmony among men, and so Huck is not much concerned with his own salvation. He repeatedly renounces prayer in favor of pragmatic solutions to his problems. In other words, the central insights of the novel belong to the tradition of the Enlightenment. The meaning of the quest itself is hardly reconcilable with that conception of human nature embodied in the myth of original sin. In view of the current fashion of reaffirming man's innate depravity, it is perhaps not surprising to find the virtues of *Huckleberry Finn* attributed not to its meaning but to its form.

But "if this was not the right ending for the book," Mr. Eliot asks, "what ending would have been right?" Although this question places the critic in an awkward position (he is not always equipped to rewrite what he criticizes), there are some things which may justifiably be said about the "right" ending of *Huckleberry Finn*. It may be legitimate, even if presumptuous, to indicate certain conditions which a hypothetical ending would have to satisfy if it were to be congruent with the rest of the novel. If the conclusion is not to be something merely tacked on to close the action, then its broad outline must be immanent in the body of the work.

It is surely reasonable to ask that the conclusion provide a plausible outcome to the quest. Yet freedom, in the ecstatic sense that Huck and Jim knew it aboard the raft, was hardly to be had in the Mississippi Valley in the 1840's, or, for that matter, in any other known human society. A satisfactory ending would inevitably cause the reader some frustration. That Clemens felt such disappointment to be inevitable is borne out by an examination of the novel's clear, if unconscious, symbolic pattern. Consider, for instance, the inferences to be drawn from the book's geography. The river, to whose current Huck and Jim entrust themselves, actually carries them to the heart of slave territory. Once the raft passes Cairo, the quest is virtually doomed. Until the steamboat smashes the raft, we are kept in a state of anxiety about Jim's escape. (It may be significant that at this point Clemens found himself unable to continue work on the manuscript, and put it aside for several years.) Beyond Cairo, Clemens allows the intensity of that anxiety to diminish, and it is probably no accident that the fainter it becomes, the more he falls back upon the devices of low comedy. Huck and Jim make no serious effort to turn north, and there are times (during the Wilks episode) when Clemens allows Huck to forget all about Jim. It is as if the author, anticipating the dilemma he had finally to face, instinctively dissipated the power of his major theme.

Consider, too, the circumscribed nature of the raft as a means of moving toward freedom. The raft lacks power and maneuverability. It can only move easily with the current—southward into slave country. Nor can it evade the mechanized power of the steamboat. These impotencies of the raft correspond to the innocent helplessness of its occupants. Unresisted, the rogues invade and take over the raft. Though it is the symbolic locus of the novel's central affirmations, the raft provides an uncertain and indeed precarious mode of traveling toward freedom. This seems another confirmation of Santayana's perception. To say that Clemens only half escaped the genteel tradition is not to say that he failed to note any of the creed's inadequacies, but rather that he had "nothing solid" to put in its place. The raft patently was not capable of carrying the burden of hope Clemens placed upon it.[6] (Whether this is to be attributed to the nature or to the actual state of American society in the nineteenth century is another interesting question.) In any case, the geography of the novel, the raft's powerlessness, the goodness and vulnerability of Huck and Jim, all prefigure a conclusion quite different in tone from that which Clemens gave us. These facts constitute what Hart Crane might have called the novel's "logic of metaphor," and this logic—probably inadvertent—actually takes us to the underlying meaning of *The Adventures of Huckleberry Finn*. Through the symbols we reach a truth which the ending obscures: the quest cannot succeed.

Fortunately, Clemens broke through to this truth in the novel's last sentences:

> But I reckon I got to light out for the territory ahead of the rest, because Aunt Sally she's going to adopt me and sivilize me, and I can't stand it. I been there before.

Mr. Eliot properly praises this as "the only possible concluding sentence." But one sentence can hardly be advanced, as Mr. Eliot advances this one, to support the rightness of ten chapters. Moreover, if this sentence is right, then the rest of the conclusion is wrong, for its meaning clashes with that of the final burlesque. Huck's decision to go west ahead of the inescapable advance of civilization is a confession of defeat. It means that the raft is to be abandoned. On the other hand, the jubilation of the family reunion and the proclaiming of Jim's freedom create a quite different mood. The tone, except for these last words, is one of unclouded success. I believe this is the source of the almost universal dissatisfaction with the conclusion. One can hardly forget that a bloody civil war did not resolve the issue.

Should Clemens have made Huck a tragic hero? Both Mr. Eliot and Mr. Trilling argue that that would have been a mistake, and they are very probably correct. But between the ending as we have it and tragedy in the fullest sense, there was vast room for invention. Clemens might have contrived an action which left Jim's fate as much in doubt as Huck's. Such an ending would have allowed us to assume that the principals were defeated but alive, and the quest unsuccessful but not abandoned. This, after all, would have been consonant with the symbols, the characters, and the theme as Clemens had created them—and with history.

Clemens did not acknowledge the truth his novel contained. He had taken hold of a situation in which a partial defeat was inevitable, but he was unable to—or unaware of the need to—give imaginative substance to the fact. If an illusion of success was indispensable, where was it to come from? Obviously Huck and Jim could not succeed by their own efforts. At this point Clemens, having only half escaped the genteel tradition, one of whose pre-eminent characteristics was an optimism undaunted by disheartening truth, returned to it. *Why* he did so is another story, having to do with his parents and his boyhood, with his own personality and his wife's, and especially with the character of his audience. But whatever the explanation, the faint-hearted ending of *The Adventures of Huckleberry Finn* remains an important datum in the record of American thought and imagination. It has been noted before, both by critics and non-professional readers. It should not be forgotten now.

To minimize the seriousness of what must be accounted a major flaw in so great a work is, in a sense, to repeat Clemens' failure of nerve. This is a disservice to criticism. Today we particularly need a criticism alert to lapses of moral vision. A measured appraisal of the failures and successes of our writers, past and present, can show us a great deal about literature and about ourselves. That is the critic's function. But he cannot perform that function if he substitutes considerations of technique for consideration of truth. Not only will such methods lead to errors of literary judgment, but beyond that, they may well encourage comparable evasions in other areas. It seems not unlikely, for instance, that the current preoccupation with matters of form is bound up with a tendency, by no means confined to literary quarters, to shy away from painful answers to complex questions of political morality. The conclusion to *The Adventures of Huckleberry Finn* shielded both Clemens and his audience from such an answer. But we ought not to be as tender-minded. For Huck Finn's besetting problem, the disparity between his best impulses and the behavior the community attempted to impose upon him, is as surely ours as it was Twain's.

[1] I use the term "genteel tradition" as George Santayana characterized it in his famous address "The Genteel Tradition in American Philosphy," first delivered in 1911 and published the following year in his *Winds of Doctrine*. Santayana described the genteel tradition as an "old mentality" inherited from Europe. It consists of the various dilutions of Christian theology and morality, as in transcendentalism—a fastidious and stale philosphy of life no longer relevant to the thought and activities of the United States. "America," he said, "is a young country with an old mentality." (Later references to Santayana also refer to this essay.)

[2] For an account of the first reviews, see A. L. Vogelback, "The Publication and Reception of *Huckleberry Finn* in America," *American Literature*, XI (November, 1939), 260-72.

[3] Mr. Eliot's essay is the introduction to the edition of *Huckleberry Finn* published by Chanticleer Press, New York, 1950. Mr. Trilling's is the introduction to an edition of the novel published by Rinehart, New York, 1948, and later reprinted in his *The Liberal Imagination*, Viking, New York, 1950.

[4] *Mark Twain at Work* (Cambridge, 1942), p. 92.

[5] For these observations on the transformation of Jim in the closing episodes, I am indebted to the excellent unpublished essay by Mr. Chadwick Hansen on the subject of Clemens and Western humor.

[6] Gladys Bellamy (*Mark Twain as a Literary Artist*, Norman, Oklahoma, 1950, p. 221) has noted the insubstantial, dream-like quality of the image of the raft. Clemens thus discusses travel by raft in *A Tramp Abroad*: "The motion of the raft is . . . gentle, and gliding, and smooth, and noiseless; it calms down all feverish activities, it sooths to sleep all nervous . . . impatience; under its restful influence all the troubles and vexations and sorrows that harass the mind vanish away, and existence becomes a dream . . . a deep and tranquil ecstasy."

Selected Criticisms

The Concord (Mass.) Public Library committee has decided to exclude Mark Twain's latest book from the library. One member of the committee says that, while he does not wish to call it immoral, he thinks it contains but little humor, and that of a very coarse type. He regards it as the veriest trash. The librarian and the other members of the committee entertain similar views, characterizing it as rough, coarse and inelegant, dealing with a series of experiences not elevating, the whole book being more suited to the slums than to intelligent, respectable people.

The Boston Transcript, March 17, 1885.

What is it that we want in a novel? We want a vivid and original picture of life; we want character naturally displayed in action, and if we get the excitement of adventure into the bargain and that adventure possible and plausible, I . . . think that we have additional cause for gratitude. If, moreover, there is an unstrained sense of humor in the narrator, we have a masterpiece, and *Huckleberry Finn* is nothing less. . . . As to the truth of the life described, the life in little innocent towns, the religion, the Southern lawlessness, the feuds, the lynchings, only persons who have known this changed world can say if it be truly painted, but it looks like the very truth, like an historical document. Already *Huckleberry Finn* is an historical novel, more valuable, perhaps, to the historian than *Uncle Tom's Cabin*, for it is written without partisanships, and without 'a purpose.'

Andrew Lang, February 14, 1891.

It is in the Mississippi Valley, however, that our author finds himself most at home, not only because his knowledge of it is more comprehensive and minutely accurate, but because it is a more congenial field. Mark Twain understands California, admires it even, but he loves the great river and the folk who dwell alongside it. He is especially happy in his delineation of the boy of this region. If ever any writer understood boy nature in general, . . . the name of that writer is Mark Twain. He has explored all its depths and shallows, and in his characters of Tom Sawyer and Huckleberry Finn he has given us such a study of the American boy as will be sought in vain elsewhere. He has done more than this; he has given us a faithful picture, painfully realistic in details, of the *ante bellum* social condition of the Mississippi Valley. This realism redeems the books from what would otherwise seem worthlessness, and gives them a positive value.

Henry C. Vedder, 1894.

But fact is unimportant in the training of a sensitive imagination, and the influence of the river upon that of Mark Twain can hardly be exaggerated.

Nor is it difficult to comprehend how it is that through whatever of his books the Mississippi flows, it fills thems with a certain portion of its power and beauty. To it is owing all that in his work which is large and fine and eloquent. The river is what makes *Huckleberry Finn* his most vivid story,. . .

Charles Miner Thompson, April, 1897.

He writes English as if it were a primitive and not a derivative language, without Gothic or Latin or Greek behind it, or German and French beside it. The result is the English in which the most vital works of English literature are cast, rather than the English of Milton and Thackerary and Mr. Henry James. I do not say that the English of the authors last named is less than vital, but only that it is not the most vital. It is scholarly and conscious; it knows who its grandfather was; it has the refinement and subtlety of an old patriciate. You will not have with it the widest suggestion, the largest human feeling, or perhaps the loftiest reach of imagination, but will have the keen joy that exquisite artistry in words can alone impart, and that you will not have in Mark Twain. What you will have in him is a style which is as personal, as biographical as the style of anyone who has written, and expresses a civilization whose courage of the chances, the preferences, the duties, is not the measure of its essential modesty. It has a thing to say, and it says it in the word that may be the first or second or third choice, but will not be the instrument of the most fastidious ear, the most delicate and exacting sense, though it will be the word that surely and strongly conveys intention from the author's mind to the reader's. It is the Abraham Lincolnian word, not the Charles Sumnerian; it is American, Western. . . .

He was the first, if not the only, man of his section to betray a consciousness of the grotesque absurdities in the Southern inversion of the civilized ideals in behalf of slavery, which must have them upside down in order to walk over them safely.

No American of Northern birth or breeding could have imagined the spiritual struggle of Huck Finn in deciding to help the negro Jim to his freedom, even though he should be forever despised as a negro thief in his native town, and perhaps eternally lost through the blackness of his sin. No Northerner could have come so close to the heart of a Kentucky feud, and revealed it so perfectly, with the whimsicality playing through its carnage, or could have so brought us into the presence of the sardonic comi-tragedy of the squalid little river town where the store-keeping magnate shoots down his drunken tormentor in the arms of the drunkard's daughter, and then cows with bitter mockery the mob that comes to lynch him. . . . Even now I think he should . . . be called a romancer, though such a book as *Huckleberry Finn* takes itself out of the order of romance and places itself with the great things in picaresque fiction. Still it is more poetic than picaresque, and of a deeper psychology. The probable and credible soul that the author divines in the son of the town drunkard is one which we might each own [as his] brother, and the art which portrays this nature at first hand in the person and language of the hero, without pose or affectation, is fine art. In the boy's history the author's fancy works realistically to an end as high as it has reached elsewhere, if not higher; and I who like *The Connecticut Yankee in King Arthur's Court* so much have half a mind to give my whole heart to *Huckleberry Finn.*

The author of *Life on the Mississippi* was also the creator of Tom Sawyer and Huck Finn, two boys who will survive to cast shame upon all the humour of America. And it is for the sake of a genuine talent that we deplore Mark Twain's studied antics. It should not have been for him to light the thorns which crackle under the pot. It should not have been for him to encourage the gross stupidity of his fellows.

. . . It is true that this incorrigible and prolific joker has kept the world chuckling so continuously that it has not sobered down to comprehend what a powerful, original thinker he is. . . . Those who are fond of classifying books may see in *Huckleberry Finn* a new specimen of the picaresque novel of adventure; some classifiers, going back further for analogies, have called it the "Odyssey of the Mississippi," which is strikingly inept. It is a piece of modern realism, original, deep and broad, and it is in American literature deplorably solitary. It is one of the unaccountable triumphs of creative power that seem to happen now and again, as *Robinson Crusoe* happened, and the surrounding intellectual territory has not its comrade.

John Macy, 1913.

But it is in *Huckleberry Finn*—the one great picaresque tale of the frontier—that the western philosophy of Mark Twain, a philosophy that derives straight from the old naturistic school, crops out most sharply. It is a drama of the struggle between the individual and the village *mores*, set in a loose picturesque framework, and exemplifying the familiar thesis that the stuff of life springs strong and wholesome from the great common stock. Huck Finn is a child of nature who has lived close to the simple facts of life, unperverted by the tyrannies of the village that would make a good boy of him. He had got his schooling from the unfenced woods, from the great river that swept past him as he idly fished, from the folk tales of negroes and poor whites, from queer adventures with Tom Sawyer; and from such experiences he had got a code of natural ethics. Then he found himself on the raft with Jim . . . , and his little pagan soul felt the stirrings of the problem of right and wrong. The village code and the natural code clashed and the conflict was terrifying.

Vernon Louis Parrington, 1930.

The title, 'The Adventures of Huckleberry Finn,' announces the structure: a picaresque novel concerned with the adventures of Huckleberry Finn. The form is the most native to Mark Twain and so best adapted to his use. . . . The lineage goes back to a native art; the novel derives from the folk and embodies their mode of thought more purely and more completely than any other ever written. The life of the south-western frontier was umbilical to the mind of Mark Twain. The blood and tissue have been formed in no other way. That life here finds issue more memorably than it has anywhere else, and since the frontier is a phase through which most of the nation has passed, the book comes nearer than any other to identify with the national life. . . . Patently, American literature has nothing to compare with it. Huck's language is a sensitive, subtle, and versatile instrument—capable of every effort it is called upon to produce. . . . It is only because the world he [Huck] passes through is real and because it is American that his journey escapes into universals and is immortal. His book is American life formed into great fiction.

Bernard DeVoto, 1932.

Huckleberry Finn starts uncertainly, achieves magnificence in the great days on the river, the feud, the killing of Boggs, and kindred episodes, then 'dies' slowly, in the tiresome, long-drawn-out account of the 'rescue'. . . . On the whole, it seems difficult to avoid accepting Arnold Bennet's judgment on both *Huck* and *Tom* that while they are 'episodically magnificent, as complete works of art they are quite inferior quality.'

Edward Wagenknecht, 1935.

A joy forever, it [*Huckleberry Finn*] is unquestionably one of the masterpieces of American and of world literature. . . . A homeless river rat, cheerful in his rags, suspicious of every attempt to civilize him, Huck has none of the unimportant virtues and all the essential ones. The school for hard knocks has taught him skepticism, horse sense, and a tenacious grasp on reality. But it has not toughened him into cynicism or crime. Nature gave him a stanch and faithful heart, friendly to all underdogs and instantly hostile toward bullies and all shapes of overmastering power. One critic has called him the type of common folk, sample of the run-of-the-mill democracy in America. Twain himself might have objected to the label, for he once declared 'there are no common people, except in the highest sphere of society.' Huck always displays a frontier neighborliness, even trying to provide a rescue for three murderers dying marooned on a wrecked boat, because 'there ain't no telling but I might come to be a murderer myself, yet, and then how would I like it?' Money does not tempt him to betray his friend Nigger Jim, though at times his conscience is troubled by the voice of convention, preaching the sacredness of property—even in the guise of flesh and blood—and he trembles on the brink of surrender. Nor can he resist sometimes the provocation offered by Jim's innocent credulity, only to be cut to the quick when his friend bears with dignity the discovery that his trustfulness has been made game of. Even as Huck surpasses Tom in qualities of courage and heart, so Nigger Jim excels even Huck in fidelity and innate manliness, to emerge as the book's noblest character.

Dixon Wecter, 1948.

Repeated readings of the book only confirm and deepen one's admiration of the consistency and perfect adaptation of the writing. This is a style which at the period, whether in America or in England, was an innovation, a new discovery in the English language. Other authors had achieved natural speech in relation to particular characters . . . but no one else had kept it up through the whole of a book. . . . In *Huckleberry Finn* there is no exaggeration of grammer or spelling or speech, there is no sentence or phrase or spelling or speech, there is no sentence or phrase to destroy the illusion that these are Huck's own words. It is not only in the way in which he tells his story, but in the details he remembers, that Huck is true to himself. . . . In *Huckleberry Finn* Mark Twain wrote a much greater book than he could have known he was writing. Perhaps all great works of art mean much more than the author could have been aware of meaning; certainly *Huckleberry Finn* is one book of Mark Twain's which, as a whole, has this unconsciousness. So what seems to be the rightness, of reverting at the end of the book to the mood of *Tom Sawyer,* was perhaps unconscious art. For Huckleberry Finn, neither a tragic nor a happy ending would be suitable. . . . Huck Finn must come from nowhere and be bound for nowhere. . . He has no beginning and no end. Hence, he can only disappear. . . . And it is as impossible for Huck as for the River to have a beginning or end—a *career.* So the book has the right, the only possible concluding sentence.''

T. S. Eliot, 1950.

Of all the characters in Mark Twain's works there probably wasn't any of whom he was fonder than the one that went down the river with Huck Finn. It is true that this character is introduced as 'Miss Watson's big nigger, named Jim.' That was the Missouri vernacular of that day. But from there on to the end of the story Miss Watson's Jim is a warm human being, lovable and admirable. Consequently it is a little odd that the New York City Board of Education should be dropping *The Adventures of Huckleberry Finn* from its approved textook lists.

The truth is that *Huckleberry Finn* is one of the deadliest satires that was ever written on some of the nonsense that goes with the inequality of the races. Who is it that flies into a rage when a free Negro from Ohio comes to town with a white shirt, a gold watch and chain and a silver-headed cane? Why it is Huck's drunken old father, who never did a stroke of work in his life if he could help it. What happens when Huck and Jim begin to argue some philosphical question? As a rule it is Jim who wins.

119

When Huck plays a mean trick on Jim and Jim's feelings are hurt, what happens? Huck goes to Jim and apologizes . . .

The mean and foolish people in this book are not Negroes. The mean and foolish people are Huck's pap and those two old frauds who are extracting money from the innocent people of 'Arkansaw' and other states by posing as the Duke of Bilgewater and the Dauphin of France. They are swindlers, members of mobs and feudists who shoot each other for nothing. They are whites. One might go so far as to say that *Huckleberry Finn* is not fair to white people. It should, nevertheless, be available for use in New York schools. One is not so certain about the Central High School of Little Rock, Ark.

New York Times, September 13, 1957.

Mark Twain's real problem—his real dilemma—was not at all his inability to "face" the issues of slavery; certainly it was not a fear of the society or a failure of moral and political courage which brought Mark Twain to the tight place where Huck had to decide forever and ever. Rather, it was the necessities of his humorous form. For in order to achieve expression of the deep wish which *Huckleberry Finn* embodies—the wish for freedom from any conscience—Mark Twain had to intensify the moral sentiment. The moment there is any real moral doubt about Huck's action, the wish will be threatened. Yet when Huck makes his moral affirmation, he fatally negates the wish for freedom from the conscience; for if his affirmation frees him from the Southern conscience, it binds him to his Northern conscience. No longer an outcast, he can be welcomed into the society to play the role of Tom Sawyer, which is precisely what happens. When he submits to Tom's role, we are the ones who become uncomfortable. The entire burlesque ending is a revenge upon the moral sentiment which, though it shielded the humor, ultimately threatened Huck's identity.

James M. Cox, 1966.

He entered his mature and later periods of writing quite triumphantly indeed, with all his old powers enhanced, rather than broken or diminished, by his own central tragic experience; by his depth realization of life's pain and evil. He retained to the end the central source of his artistic virtue: that untouched spring of pagan, plenary, and edenic innocence, that full sense of joy and pleasure in life, which sprang up even more freely in his final decades—which came to a second and later flowering despite all those civilizational discontents which he, perhaps more than any other American writer, also felt so directly and personally at the center of his being.

It was only certain Twain critics, from the youthful Van Wyck Brooks, who came to change his mind, to Bernard De Voto and Charles Neider and Justin Kaplan, . . . who refused to acknowledge—or who were perhaps ignorant of—the value of his later writing. Mark Twain was more correct in his own estimate of that work, his joy in writing it, and yes, his pleasure in receiving the world's acclamation then (and yet again today) for having written it. The last periods of his writing were indeed younger in spirit if wiser in essence than much of his earlier and middle periods of work. *Huck Finn* as his single great classic—what nonsense! His whole career was a classic. He was not merely the artist of American youth and the past; he was surely our most mature and wisest of artists whose acerbity and profundity alike were ringed about with the imperishable comic spirit. In his age he only became freer, bolder, more open and honest, more emancipated both socially and sexually, from the taboos of his epoch which, at base, his spirit had never accepted.

Maxwell Geisman, 1970.

Bibliography

Alter, Robert. *Rogue's Progress: Studies in the Picaresque Novel*. Cambridge, Mass.: Harvard University Press, 1964.

Auden, W. H. "Huck and Oliver," *Listener*, L. (October 1953).

Banta, Martha. "Rebirth or Revenge: The Endings of *Huckleberry Finn* and *The American*." *Modern Fiction Studies, XV (1969)*.

Barchilon, José, and Joel S. Kovel. "*Huckleberry Finn*: A Psychoanalytic Study." *Journal of the American Psychoanalytic Assoc.*, XIV (1966).

Barnes, Daniel R. "Twain's *The Adventures of Huckleberry Finn*, Chapter I." *Explicator*, XXIII (April, 1965).

Berkove, Lawrence I. "Language and Literature: The 'Poor Players' of *Huckleberry Finn*." Papers of the Michigan Academy of Science, Arts, and Letters, LIII (1968).

Bernadete, Jane J. "*Huckleberry Finn* and the Nature of Fiction." *Massachusetts Review*, IX (Spring, 1968).

Blair, Walter. *Mark Twain and Huck Finn*. Berkeley: University of California Press, 1960.

————. "When Was *Huckleberry Finn* Written?" *American Literature*, XXX (March, 1958).

Branch, Edgar M. "The Two Providences: Thematic Form in *Huckleberry Finn*." *College English*, XI (January, 1950).

Burns, Graham. "Time and Pastoral; *The Adventures of Huckleberry Finn*." *Critical Review*, XV (1972).

Cox, James M. "Remarks on the Sad Initiation of Huckleberry Finn." *Sewanee Review*, LXII (Summer, 1954).

Fiedler, Leslie, *Love and Death in the American Novel*. New York: Criterion, 1960.

Frantz, Ray W., Jr. "The Role of Folklore in *Huckleberry Finn*." *American Literature*, XXVIII (November, 1956).

Fraser, John. "In Defense of Culture: *Huckleberry Finn*." *Oxford Review*, VI (1967).

Gullason, Thomas A. "The 'Fatal' Ending of *Huckleberry Finn*." *American Literature*, XXIX (March, 1957).

Hansen, Chadwick. "The Character of Jim and the Ending of *Huckleberry Finn*." *Massachusetts Review*, V (Autumn, 1963).

Lane, Lauriat, Jr. "Why *Huckleberry Finn* Is a Great World Novel." *College English*, XVII (October, 1955).

Leary, Lewis. "Tom and Huck: Innocence on Trial." *Virginia Quarterly Review*, XXX (Summer, 1954).

Levy, Leo. B. "Society and Conscience in *Huckleberry Finn*." *Nineteenth-Century Fiction*, XVIII (March, 1964).

Lynn, Kenneth S. "Huck and Jim." *Yale Review*, XLVII (Spring, 1958).

Manierre, William R. "On Keeping the Raftsmen's Passage in *Huckleberry Finn*." *English Language Notes*, VI (1968).

Moses, W. R. "The Pattern of Evil in *Adventures of Huckleberry Finn*." *Georgia Review*, XIII (Summer, 1959).

O'Connor, William Van. " Why *Huckleberry Finn* Is Not the Great American Novel." *College English*, XVII (October, 1955).

Rubenstein, Gilbert M. "The Moral Structure of *Huckleberry Finn*." *College English*, XVIII (November, 1956).

Rubin, Louis D., Jr. "Mark Twain and the Language of Experience." *Sewanee Review*, LXXI (Autumn, 1963).

Schmitz, Neil. "The Paradox of Liberation in *Huckleberry Finn*." *Texas Studies in Literature and Language*, XIII (1971).

———. "Twain, *Huckleberry Finn*, and the Reconstruction." *American Studies*, XII (Spring, 1971).

Trachtenberg, Alan. "The Form of Freedom in *Adventures of Huckleberry Finn*." *Southern Review* (Autumn, 1970).

Vales, Robert L. "Thief and Theft in *Huckleberry Finn*." *American Literature*, XXXVII (January, 1966).

Vogelback, Arthur L. "The Publication and Reception of *Huckleberry Finn* in America." *American Literature*, XI (November, 1939).

Yates, Norris W. "The 'Counter-Conversion' of Huckleberry Finn." *American Literature*, XXXII (March, 1960).

Young, Philip. "*Adventures of Huckleberry Finn*." In *Ernest Hemingway*. New York: Rinehart, 1952.

NOTES